SCHIRMER PERFORMANCE EDITIONS

HANON
THE VIRTUOSO PIANIST
Complete

T0071724

based on the original edition
translated from French

with historical and pedagogical notes
by Matthew Edwards

On the cover:
Young Man Playing the Piano (1876)
by Gustave Caillebotte
(1848–1894)

ISBN: 978-1-4803-6737-1

G. SCHIRMER, *Inc.*

DISTRIBUTED BY

HAL•LEONARD®
CORPORATION
7777 W. BLUEMOUND RD. P.O. BOX 13819 MILWAUKEE, WI 53213

www.musicsalesclassical.com
www.halleonard.com

CONTENTS

PART ONE

Preparatory Exercises for the Acquirement of Agility, Independence, Strength and Perfect Evenness in the Fingers

PART TWO

Transcendent Exercises for Preparing the Fingers for the Virtuoso Exercises

PART THREE

Virtuoso Exercises for Obtaining a Mastery over the Greatest Mechanical Difficulties

HISTORICAL AND PEDOGOGICAL NOTES

History

In the nineteenth century, in a relatively obscure corner of France, a musician set about writing a few short exercises, intending to assist his students as they sought to improve their skills at the piano. As he put his pen to the page, Charles Louis Hanon could not possibly have guessed that this work would become the most widely known collection of exercises in the entire piano repertoire. From Seoul to Salzburg, from Baltimore to Berlin, students and teachers across the globe have utilized these rudimentary works in their pursuit of virtuosity.

Born in northern France in 1819, Hanon's early career and publications are, appropriately, rooted in pedagogy. Being a deeply religious man, his first important publication was a method for accompanying plainchant on the organ, entitled *Système nouveau*. So great was its success that he was recognized by Pope Pius IX, and given an Honorable Mention at the World Exhibition in Paris in 1867.

The 1860s saw the publication of many of his works for piano, but it was in 1874 that he published that which would bring him the most fame, *The Virtuoso Pianist*. The original, complete French title is *Le Pianiste virtuose en 60 exercices, calculés pour acquérir l'agilité, l'indépendance, la force et la plus parfaite égalité des doigts ainsi que la souplesse des poignets* (The Virtuoso Pianist in 60 Exercises, calculated to gain agility, independence, strength, and perfect equality in the fingers and flexibility in the wrist.) Hanon notes in the preface that with a few exceptions, the work is entirely his own composition. Those exceptions are some exercises borrowed from *Etudes pour le piano* by Aloys Schmitt (1788–1866).

Initially released as a single volume, *The Virtuoso Pianist* was later positioned as the third book in a four-volume set, entitled *Elementary Method for the Piano*. Volume one was a primer in music reading and technique, while volumes two and four were collections of pieces to study—the last consisted exclusively of works by Hanon himself, all corresponding directly to the exercises of *The Virtuoso Pianist*. Ultimately, the other three volumes separated from the set, and *The Virtuoso Pianist* soon stood alone once again.

The book has undeniably served as a help to generations of pianists, both beginners and advanced. In fact, it was at one time the centerpiece of technical instruction at the Moscow Conservatory. To quote Sergei Rachmaninoff, when he wrote about the conservatory's program:

> During the first five years the student gets most of his technical instruction from a book of studies by Hanon, which is used very extensively in the conservatories. In fact this is practically the only book of strictly technical studies employed.

Many editions have been released, including its biggest selling edition, the English translation which was released by G. Schirmer in 1900. For this new Schirmer Performance Editions version, *The Virtuoso Pianist* has been re-researched and given new music engraving, making it crisp and easy to read, as well as adding historical and pedagogical articles.

Hanon would never see the incredible success and impact of the Schirmer edition, for he died in that same year, on March 19, 1900. After his passing, a church publication remembered him thus:

> Charles Hanon was one of those Christians of old stock such as we rarely encounter today. He always gave generously to the poor, and he sustained a multitude of Catholic charities [as well as] expelled monks and impoverished artists. His piety was exemplary. He was seen at mass daily, and he took Holy Communion each morning. It was at church that he caught [the pneumonia] that caused his death a few days later.

Though his obituary would reflect the simple life of a common man, this single volume of exercises went on to touch more musicians than one could possibly hope to count.

Thoughts and Observations on Using the Exercises

In doing research for this preface I polled several teachers and pianists about the ways in which they incorporated *The Virtuoso Pianist* into their teaching and practice. A great majority of teachers utilized only portions of it; in particular and not surprisingly, the first twenty exercises. Others use the scale fingerings as a reference. Few teachers have taught Exercise 60 at all.

Opinions today about Hanon's exercises and their use are countless. It is important, therefore, to read Hanon's original preface, included in this edition. Although not extensively detailed, it serves to reveal his general intent and motivations for the ordering of the exercises.

With Hanon's preface in mind, perhaps the set of exercises should not always be practiced piecemeal, but rather in a linear fashion, moving in order from exercise to exercise. A careful look at the book as a whole reveals the preface's point of a general progression of the technique toward certain goals. Hanon's order indeed has a purpose.

Certainly the first 38 exercises lead, in nearly a straight line, to scale practice. The early rudimentary exercises address speed, clarity, and evenness—critical elements for scales and other passages. Following the rudiments are the studies on finger crossings, allowing the student to isolate and perfect this concept. Then, when arriving at the scale exercises, the only "new" topics are fingerings and key signatures. Many of the other important aspects of scale practice have already been addressed.

Once the scales have been accomplished, many of the greater difficulties of piano playing are touched on in the later exercises, particularly double notes and octaves. This is a very logical next step in the progression of one's technique.

Admittedly, it would be a fairly advanced student who could reach the point of playing through the book in an hour, as Hanon recommends in his preface. However, a student who stays the course at least through the scale sections could indeed, with proper guidance, significantly improve technique by playing the exercises in order regularly up through the scales.

Lastly, it should be noted that the primary goals of practicing this set should include clarity, steadiness of rhythm, and evenness of tone.

The Exercises

Exercises 1–20
Short Rudimentary Ascent and Descent

"The exercises are so arranged, that in each successive number the fingers are rested from the fatigue caused by the one preceding."

—Charles Louis Hanon

Part One presents the basic, introductory rudiments, the best-known portion of the *The Virtuoso Pianist*. The first six notes of the scale (with a couple of exceptions) are presented in various combinations. The student can begin to develop rapidity, agility, clarity, and to some extent, independence of the fingers.

Each of the twenty exercises has a specific purpose, and Hanon indicates this in a brief note before each exercise. Teachers may find these instructions (such as, "For stretching the 4th and 5th fingers, and exercising the five fingers") useful if choosing specific exercises to correspond to other music the student is working on. Throughout these first twenty exercises, clarity and evenness are the two most important goals on which to focus, foundational to good technique.

As an alternative to practicing all twenty in order, some of them could be grouped by similarity in purpose. Students may learn the exercises faster if grouped in such a way; it may also help concentrate the focus on specific types of finger movement. Although several options exist, one suggestion for grouping is given here:

Exercises 1–3
Exercises 4–6, 12, 16, 19
Exercises 7–9, 17, 18
Exercises 10–11, 14
Exercises 13, 15
Exercises 20

Exercises 21–30
Extended Rudimentary Ascent and Descent

Although the original edition warns that Part Two, beginning Exercise 21, should not be practiced until Part One is well-prepared and studied, these exercises may initially seem simply like longer versions of the first twenty exercises. Many of the same figurations are contained here, but by doubling the length of the pattern, Hanon is able to expand and elaborate, extending the note pattern from two beats in Part One to four beats in Part Two.

Exercise 31 is a transitional exercise, following the basic pattern of the previous ones, but leading into exercises that focus on preparing the student for scale work.

Exercises 32–36
Thumb/Crossing Exercises and Scale Preparation

Good exercises for crossing the thumb under ascending or the finger over the thumb descending with the second, third, fourth, and—yes—fifth fingers. Needless to say crossings involving fingers 2, 3, and 4 are common, and the exercises prove quite helpful in preparing for scales. Some may find some of these thumb crossings tiring to practice. I would advise particular caution with Exercises 32 and 35.

Exercise 32 is such a persistent reiteration of thumb and second, that it is possible to unnecessarily tire the thumb if played with tension. The tension itself may be an indicator of something that needs technical attention. If it can be practiced in a very relaxed manner, with as little tension as possible, Exercise 32 is beneficial. Exercises 33 and 34 provide the most obvious and necessary preparation for scales.

It is interesting that in the original edition, Hanon states that Exercise 35 is "...of the highest importance." While crossings involving the fifth finger and thumb can be found in piano literature, they are surely the least common of all. The difficulty here is in maintaining any kind of proper hand position while repeating the crossings at every scale degree. In particular, when approaching the turnaround at the high point of the pattern, the pianist will surely find it to be one of the most awkward positions ever to find oneself in at the keyboard. However, perhaps becoming comfortable and fluent with these unusual positions was Hanon's point.

Exercise 36 rehearses the thumb crossing in yet another variation; this type of crossing is common, and the reiterations here provide a good opportunity to perfect it.

Exercise 37
Passing the Thumb. Special Exercise

I would advise caution in studying and teaching this exercise. The chord is held with the second, fourth, and fifth fingers, while the thumb plays notes below and between those fingers. If the thumbs playing the quarter notes can possibly strike the keys in a relaxed manner, and the fingers holding the silent notes can do so without tension, then this could provide some benefit. However, more often than not, the chord is held down with unnecessary force, causing additional strain on the thumbs.

Exercise 38
Exercise for preparing to study the scales

This is the perfect final transition into the scale section. Essentially, it is a rudiment that reinforces the C-major fingering as it ascends and descends, using the white notes exclusively. It may be advisable to practice the contrary motion portion of this first, as students may more quickly learn the fingering when it is a mirror image, and is the "same" in each hand, with the thumb crossing under on the fourth note of the pattern after the third finger.

Exercises 39–40
Major, Minor, and Chromatic Scales

At last, the arrival of the scales. If the student has indeed covered the preceding exercises thoroughly, mastering the fingerings should be the primary challenge. A thorough study of the earlier exercises should have already helped the student achieve clarity, evenness and speed.

The scales are laid out according to the circle of fifths, moving through the flat keys first, then down through the sharps. Each major scale is presented with its relative minor, in both the harmonic and melodic forms. Each scale closes with a grand harmonic cadence. I certainly prefer the cadential format shown here, as it seems more practical and more likely to be encountered than smaller triadic formulas often presented in student material.

As an alternative to the cadence, the single note scales can be connected together using the device seen at the end of each of the scales in octaves in Exercise 53.

The fingerings, which may have simply been in practice and documented by Hanon, are the same ones that countless teachers and students have used for many years; there seems little real need to consider any other scale fingerings.

The extensive work on the chromatic scale may seem unusual for today, but can provide a good opportunity to practice the hands being precisely together. And one does encounter chromatic scales in literature occasionally. Again, the fingerings are standard, with one variation given at the end of the section, suggested as an alternative for more legato playing.

Exercises 41–43
Arpeggios

Root position triadic arpeggios in major keys and their relative minor keys, diminished seventh-chord arpeggios, and dominant-seventh arpeggios are all presented in this section. The key scheme for the triad arpeggios is the same as for the scales, in a circle of fifths. Fingerings are once again fairly standard, but some small variations could be considered. As a single example, some may choose to use finger 3 instead of 4 in the left hand for the second note of the arpeggio in some of the keys.

In many respects, the central difficulty of arpeggios is the thumb cross under going up or finger cross over the thumb going down. While it has been studied extensively to this point in the set, the greater distance between the notes in arpeggios creates a very different challenge. Most commonly, students will respond to that interval distance by swinging the elbow outward, as the wrist twists to reach the next note. Both of these actions can hinder the speed of the arpeggio, as well as potentially muddy its execution. Keep the hand moving right through the ascent and descent of the arpeggio. Try to think of it as the hand taking the fingers to the notes, rather than the fingers reaching for the notes.

That last statement is particularly true for the diminished-seventh and dominant-seventh arpeggios. If the fingers "reach out" for the notes, they spread out into what can be an uncomfortable position. Again, keep the hand moving over the notes, so the fingers can play each in the most comfortable way.

Exercises 44–47
Repeated Notes and Trills

These can be helpful exercises, isolating two frequently encountered elements of piano technique. On the repeated-note exercises, Hanon's recommendation for the fingers to be lifted high, without raising the hand and wrist comes from his perspective of building "finger strength." I would instead suggest flexibility in the wrist/hand as the fingers are "dropped" into the keys.

Exercise 45 stands halfway between the repeated note and trill exercises, providing practice for each. The "6th fingering" may prove the most challenging.

Nearly every possible combination of single-note trills is found in Exercise 46. Practice these with a slight rotation of the hand/wrist, and not with the fingers exclusively. Of particular interest are the two examples from Mozart and Thalberg. The latter is a very effective fingering, spreading the trill over three fingers instead of just two.

Exercises 48–51
Wrist Exercise. Double Notes, Repeated and Scale Preparation

Exercises 48 and 51 are excellent preparations for scales in octaves and passages with repetitive intervals. The wrist must indeed be flexible, and the arm relaxed. Raising the hand high may be a good initial practice, when training the basic motion, but a smaller hand motion will become necessary as the speed increases. As Hanon says, the fingers should indeed be firm but not stiff (or tense).

For Exercise 49, keep the focus on the smooth and even rotation of each interval. It may be a good idea to practice the second half of this exercise first, as it may prove to be slightly less difficult than the first half because of the change in pattern in measure 4 of the first half. Because of this, the second half could be practiced with a consistent fingering throughout, such as 1-4, then 2-5.

Exercise 50 is appropriately placed. The technique needed for fingered double note passages does indeed lie somewhere between legato scale technique and that of the repeated figures in number 48. While the fingers must be active, the hand/wrist must also be flexible, so as not to invite tension in these difficult passages. After all, Hanon included Exercise 50 in the section labeled "Wrist Exercise." The first portion isolates portions of scales in double thirds in a five-finger position, helping the pianist focus on the essential technique without concern for scale fingerings. A single caution in the "Scales in Legato Thirds" section: hold the fifth finger (or thumb) down loosely, not with great pressure. The goal here is simply to connect the scale in as legato a manner as possible.

Exercise 51, with emphasis on wrist flexibility, is challenging yet excellent preparation for playing scales in octaves (Exercise 53).

Exercises 52–53
Double note scales, Thirds and Octaves

These scales in thirds and octaves are certainly challenging, but are a critical element for anyone striving for advanced technical command of the keyboard. The scales in thirds are well worth the effort involved in learning the fingerings. The previous few exercises are definitely helpful when approaching Exercises 52–53.

Hanon presents only a portion of the total number of scales ("in the Keys Most Used"), choosing to give us the major scales up to four sharps or flats, and only three minor scales. Students who master the keys here would be encouraged to learn the scales in the remaining keys.

Just as single-note scales typically are based on recurring sets of 1-2-3 and 1-2-3-4, double-third scales tend to include recurring sets of 3-4-5 and 2-3-4-5. There are some differences of opinion as to where the second finger should be placed, at least in the case of those scales that are similar to C major. Hanon's suggestion most often is for the 2 to be in the lower half of the scale; essentially, the 2-3-4-5 comes before the 3-4-5. However, this is not always the case, for depending on the location of sharps or flats, he may choose to put the 2-3-4-5 set second. As a result, sometimes Hanon's fingerings presented here do not seem as consistent as they could be.

All 24 scales in octaves are presented next. Hanon insists on proper wrist movement when practicing these. As stated before, an exaggerated raising and dropping of the octave into the keys may prove helpful initially at slow tempos, but the motion will become less prominent, although still observably present, as the speed increases.

Hanon also states that the fourth finger of either hand should be used for the black keys. In my opinion the fourth finger on a black key will indeed be more comfortable, but not necessarily every time.

An important feature of these octave scales is the connection made when progressing from one to the next in the order given. I refer to this as the "turnaround," and it allows the scales to flow uninterrupted from C major all the way to the end on E minor. I recommend this order as an option for single-note scales as well.

Exercises 54–55
Double and Triple note trills

While trills such as these may not be exceedingly common, this practice can still potentially improve the dexterity and clarity of playing double notes of any kind at high speed. Hanon's unique fingerings at the end of Exercise 55 cover yet a few more options that may be encountered in larger works.

Exercises 56–57
Broken and Arpeggiated Octaves

For the broken octaves, keep the middle of the hand centered over each successive octave, allowing the hand to rotate over that point, essentially as when playing a stationary tremolo. As the hand moves up the scale, the rotation continues.

The arpeggiated octaves in Exercise 57 are quite difficult. Slow practice is obviously recommended, but pay particularly close attention to the movement of the hand/arm as you play the octaves. In other words, one should practice how to arrive at the correct notes, almost in a slow-motion version of full speed. If the metronome clicks slowly, but we move between the notes quickly, we incorporate a pause before playing that simply will not be possible at full tempo.

Exercise 58
Sustained Octaves

Be sure to hold the octaves down loosely, without tension. Very little weight is required to keep the keys depressed. As a result, the fingers playing the interior repeated notes will be less likely to become tense or tight.

Exercise 59
Quadruple Trills in Sixths

Hanon advises that neither hand nor wrist should be moved during this exercise; however, doing so puts the complete burden of this onto the fingers alone. An alternate suggestion would be a supple wrist, and a hand that can adjust slightly to balance over each interval.

Exercise 60
Tremolo

The last of the set, Exercise 60 is surely the most difficult; there is a sense that being able to play this work indeed places one into the "Virtuoso" category of pianists. Of all the exercises in this set, this one has the most potential for exhaustion, so it should be approached carefully. Correct and balanced rotation should be the focus at all times.

Alternative Practice of the Exercises

For as long as I can remember, I have heard suggestions for practicing the first thirty exercises in alternative ways. To mention just a few:

Altered rhythm. Usually this method involves a pattern of dotted 8th note followed by a 16th note, or the reverse, either as "long-short," or "short-long." Some teachers believe that by emphasizing this rhythm, evenness and speed will be more attainable when returning to the running sixteenth notes.

Another version of this idea of altering the rhythm is to pause on a pitch after playing a predetermined number of notes. For example, playing the first four notes of a measure as 32nd notes, tied to an 8th note, then on beat two the next four notes as 32nd notes, tied to an 8th note, etc.

Changing articulations. The typical rehearsal of these exercises is with legato, although *portato* or *staccato* practice could also be useful, especially when returning to legato afterwards. One of my early piano teachers asked me to practice the exercises one hand staccato and one hand legato. I found this extremely helpful for control of articulation, and for independence of the hands.

Yet another possibility is the "drop-lift" of the two-note slur. In this approach the first two 16th notes would be slurred, then the next two 16th notes, etc.

Changing dynamics. Though the goal of the book is technique, it is useful to incorporate at least some consideration of dynamics, in particular crescendos and decrescendos. This is especially true since the ability to play evenly and clearly at all levels of dynamics is a technical accomplishment. So an exercise might be played *f*, *mf*, *mp*, or *p*. Consider a crescendo from the beginning to the peak (measure 15 in Exercise 1, for instance), and a decrescendo on the entire descent. Or vice versa. Likewise, it is possible to use crescendo and decrescendo at smaller intervals; half the ascent, or two measures, etc.

A further challenge is to play opposite dynamics, or opposite crescendos and decrescendos between the hands. This is another excellent practice for independence of the hands.

Alternate keys. I have heard many people suggest this as an option; practicing the exercises in D Major, E Major, C-sharp Major, or any of the other keys could certainly prove to be a challenge. The student will either memorize the exercise and move it to another key, or learn to transpose at sight. Certainly, doing so could reinforce the fluency in different keys and build theoretical mastery. In some keys the fingering of the original key will likely need adjustments.

Tempo changes. It is common for a teacher to ask a student to play a Hanon exercise at various steady tempos, be they slow and deliberate or fast and fluent. Hanon himself indicated a wide range of metronome markings for each exercise. Differing the tempo makes one aware of the physical movement from note to note in various ways.

Misunderstandings of The Virtuoso Pianist

Despite the fact that *The Virtuoso Pianist* is by far the most used set of piano finger exercises in the world, and many swear by its effectiveness, there are also those who loathe finger exercises in general in every way. Some opinions encountered:

The Exercises Are Boring? We must remember that performance is not the intent of finger exercises. Few would say that doing calisthenics is interesting or exciting; yet most would agree that they can be a healthy practice with great benefits. Most typically, a piano finger exercise isolates a specific or general type of technique, and allows the pianist to focus only on that, nothing more. Some students need to be reminded that patient and persistent practice of anything, including Hanon, gives rich rewards.

The Exercises May Cause Injury? First, it is important to remember that nearly any work or exercise for piano has the potential to be injurious, if it is practiced improperly. Second, one should always be observant of how one's fingers/hands/ arms are responding physically, not only to exercises, but to *any* piano music that is studied. Concerns exist over repetitive stress/strain injuries in a work built on repetition, as Hanon. But the study of repetitive rudiments and exercises could actually help us focus on playing properly, avoiding injury, and could prepare a student for better repetitive practice in larger works.

Teacher guidance is of the utmost importance. As teachers, we cannot simply say "Do the next Hanon exercise for next week," and move on to the other music in the lesson. We must guide students through the best ways to physically approach the exercises, so they receive the maximum benefit possible, and understand what they are trying to accomplish in practice.

"High Fingers?" At the end of his instructions on the very first exercise, Hanon states that the student should "Lift the fingers high and with precision." Who knows exactly what he meant

by this instruction? From all his other comments, we know he did not mean to create deliberate tension. I believe one must be extremely careful not to focus exclusively on the fingers as the sole "activators" of the keys. Doing so has a tendency, in my experience and observations, to bring about tension and exhaustion far more quickly. A better approach would be to allow the fingers to drop into the keys, as a more relaxed hand and wrist move the fingers to each note. It should feel like all parts are involved—finger, hand, wrist, arm—but without the tension of grasping at the notes, almost in a plucking manner.

The first twenty exercises can be the best place to train the movement of the hand and wrist, as each are within a small specific range, and allow the student to focus on relaxed movement in a small pattern. Since the figures all essentially begin and end with the thumb or fifth finger, there is a natural circle or rotation that will be made with the hand.

Final Thoughts

Of course, my preface to this edition can only serve to advise caution, encourage research when approaching technical studies, and to provide a few tips where possible. It is far beyond the scope of these paragraphs to detail all of the problems and solutions of piano technique. Although not every pianist who practices from this book will

become a virtuoso, anyone who studies it will find improvements in technique.

If this is your first acquaintance with Hanon, I trust that it will be a rewarding study, in which you will find challenges and successes that lead you to a higher plane as a pianist. If you have had many years of experience with Hanon, and the "newness" of his work has worn off, I trust that the thoughts presented here may help you to see these exercises and Hanon's intentions from a new perspective.

What we do as teachers does affect those we teach, in lasting and permanent ways. After all, *The Virtuoso Pianist* was born out of Hanon's simple desire to help his own students. He didn't realize he would also help millions of others.

—Matthew Edwards

Citations

Charles Timbrell, "Who Was Hanon?"
Piano and Keyboard (May/June 1995): 31.

Andre Adams and Bradley Martin,
"Charles Louis Hanon's Life and Works."
American Music Teacher (June/July 2009): 18–21.

Laurence H. Morton, "Hanon, The Virtuoso Pianist: Rotation Principle."
Unpublished manuscript (ca. 1987).

HANON'S ORIGINAL PREFACE

1874

Translated from French

The study of the piano is so prevalent these days, and good pianists are so plentiful today on this instrument, that we no longer tolerate mediocrity. The result is that we must study piano eight or ten years before venturing to play a piece of a certain difficulty, even for fellow amateurs. How few people are able to devote so many years to the study of this instrument! So it often happens that for lack of sufficient practice the execution is uneven and few play decently. The left hand fails to execute in most somewhat difficult passages, the 4th and 5th finger are almost useless, for lack of specific exercises for these fingers, which are always weaker than the others; and if we encounter some passages in octaves, trills or tremolo, they are executed with difficulty and fatigue, the result being incorrect and without expression.

For several years we worked to eliminate this situation, seeking to abstract in one book special exercises which allow for comprehensive studies for the piano in a lot less time. To achieve this goal, it is sufficient to find the solution of the following problem:

> *If the five fingers of each of our hands were quite equally exercised, they would be able to execute all that has been written for this instrument, and fingering would be the only problem before us, and that solution could quickly be found.*

We solved this problem by our book: *The Virtuoso Pianist in 60 Exercises*, etc. We find in this volume, the exercises necessary to acquire agility. The independence, strength and most perfect equality of the fingers, and the flexibility of the wrists are all indispensable qualities to arrive at a beautiful execution; moreover, these exercises have been calculated so that the left hand becomes as fluent as the right hand. Apart from a few exercises that are found in several methods, all the rest of the book is our personal invention. These exercises are interesting and do not tire the student as most five finger exercises, and do not have the dryness that takes a real artist to have the courage to explore them with such perseverance.

We have composed these exercises so that after having seen them a few times, you can play them with fairly rapid movement so that they are excellent practice for the fingers, so that the student does not lose one does not lose one moment in progressing.

Different pianists can freely play all these exercises on several pianos at once, giving emulation to students, and accustoming them to playing in ensemble.

We meet in this volume all kinds of difficulties. We have arranged the exercises in such a way that in any exercise tired fingers are resting from the previous exercise. The result of this combination, which is executed without effort or fatigue, addresses all the difficulties of the mechanism; and after this work the fingers feel amazing ease of implementation.

This book is intended for all student pianists. As soon as we study about a year, we can work it with great success. As for those more advanced, they will study in a short time, and then will no longer feel the stiffness in the fingers or wrists, which will enable them to perform the great mechanical difficulties.

The pianists and teachers who do not have enough time to practice to maintain their skills would only need to play the exercises for a few hours to find all the agility of their fingers.

Play this complete volume in an hour; and once you have it perfectly, if one repeats the task every day for some time, difficulties will disappear as if by magic, and beautiful, clear execution will happen, precise and pearly, which is the secret of distinguished artists. Finally we present this book as giving the key to all the problems of the mechanism. Also, we believe we render a real service to young pianists, teachers and school mistresses, by offering to adopt for their students our book, *The Virtuoso Pianist*.

—Charles Louis Hanon

THE VIRTUOSO PIANIST

PART ONE

*Preparatory Exercises for the Acquirement of Agility, Independence,
Strength and Perfect Evenness in the Fingers*

Part One

Charles Louis Hanon

For the stretch from the 5th to the 4th finger of the left hand in ascension (part A), and the stretch from the 5th to the 4th finger in the right hand in descension (part B). For the twenty exercises of Part One we will begin with a metronome marking of quarter note = 60 and progressively increase to quarter note = 108. The double metronome indication at the start of each exercise is to be understood in this way.

Articulate each finger so that each note is heard very distinctly.

*Once this exercise is mastered, go on to Exercise 2 without stopping on the final note.

Note that in everything in this volume both hands constantly perform the same difficulties; the left hand will manage to be as skillful as the right hand. In addition, difficulties performed by the left hand in ascending are exactly reproduced by the same fingers of the right hand in descending. This new kind of exercise will cause both hands to acquire perfect equality.

Fingers to be trained: 3, 4. Once this exercise is mastered, the preceding one and this one should be played several times without interruption, and without stiffness. The fingers will strengthen considerably by practice. This advice should be observed for the subsequent exercises.

The fourth and fifth fingers are naturally weak. This exercise and the following ones up to No. 31 are intended to make them as strong and agile as the second and third fingers.

Fingers to be trained: 2, 3, 4. Before beginning Exercise 3, once or twice, if possible, play without stopping the previous two exercises. When this third exercise can be played properly, number 4 may be studied and then number 5, and as they have been learned perfectly, play through all three at least four times continuously without interruption, stopping only on the last note of the fourth exercise. The entire volume should be practiced in this way. When playing the exercises of Part One stop only on the last note of exercises 2, 5, 8, 11, 14, 17 and 20.*

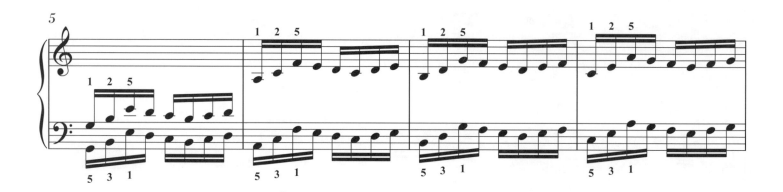

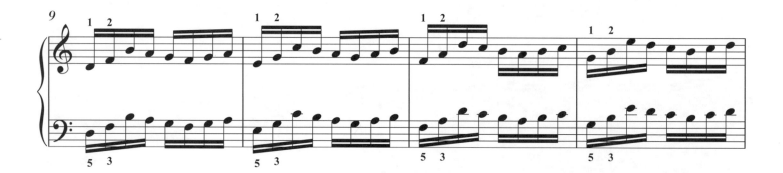

*However, it is to be feared that fatigue will be revealed by a tightening of the wrist during those successive executions. In this case, it would be harmful not to stop; on the contrary, one should stop immediately.

Any piano technique is based on flexibility without which most conscientious work becomes sterile and even harmful. Flexibility is the essential basis of all physical exercise: a swimmer who tenses is doomed to drowning, and in the field of fencing, the fencer without wrist flexibility is at the mercy of his opponent. This truth is known to all athletes.

Or if music is a reflection of the heart, sensitivity, intelligence and culture, both from the creators and the interpreters, the fact remains that performing musicians (pianists, violinists, cellists, etc.) are all tributaries of their muscles and the natural laws that govern our bodies are only valid.

Therefore, we cannot overstate that it is crucial for a pianist to achieve the total flexibility of the hand, wrist, arm and shoulder. And while it is essential to articulate fingers in working slowly and loudly, it is also essential to reduce the articulation, and loudness, as soon as rapidity increases, and this in inverse proportion to the acceleration, in order to avoid the dangerous tension which will certainly manifest if this recommendation is neglected.

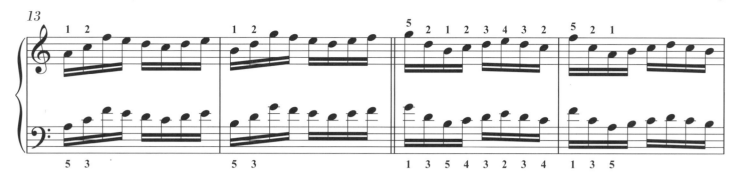

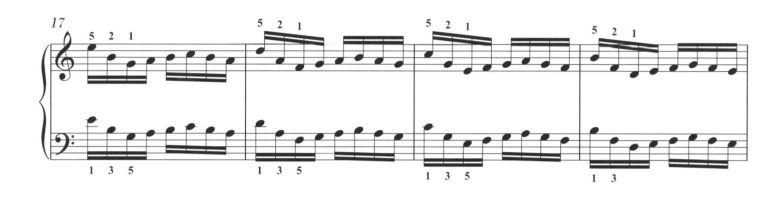

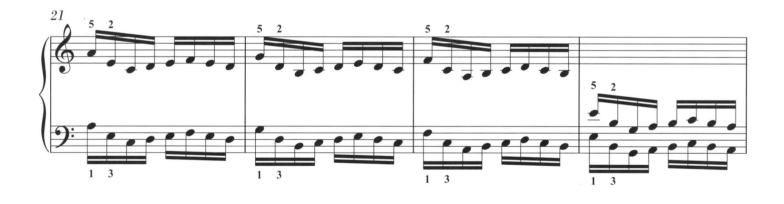

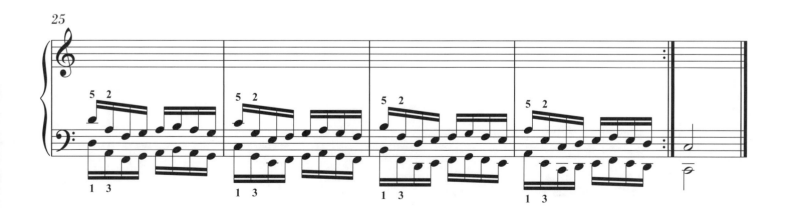

6

Fingers to be trained: 3, 4, 5. A special exercise for the 3rd, 4th and 5th fingers of the left hand.

Fingers to be trained: 1, 2, 3, 4, 5. We believe it is always necessary to repeat that the fingers need to be well articulated until this entire volume has been mastered (see the footnote on the previous exercise).

*Preparatory exercise to learning the trill, for the 4th and 5th fingers of the right hand.

8

Finger to be trained: 5. To get the right results promised to the students of this book, it is essential to play at least once every day the exercises already learned.

Fingers to be trained: 3, 4, 5. This exercise is of great importance for the 3rd, 4th and 5th fingers.

Fingers to be trained: 1, 2, 3, 4, 5. This exercise is very important for the five fingers.

For stretching the 4th and 5th fingers, and exercising the five fingers.

Fingers to be trained: 3, 4. Preparation for the trill, for the 3rd and 4th fingers of the left hand ascending, and the 3rd and 4th fingers of the right hand descending.

Fingers to be trained: 3, 4, 5. Another preparation exercise for the trill for the 4th and 5th fingers.

14

For stretching the 1st and 5th fingers, and exercising 3, 4 and 5.

Fingers to be trained: 3, 4, 5.

Fingers to be trained: 3, 4. Another preparation for the trill for the 3rd and 4th fingers.

For stretching the 1st and 2nd fingers, and exercising the five fingers.

For stretching the 3rd and 5th fingers, and exercising the 3rd, 4th and 5th fingers.

For stretching between 1 and 2, 2 and 4, and 4 and 5, and exercising 3, 4 and 5.

20

Fingers to be trained: 1, 2, 3, 4, 5.

Fingers to be trained: 1, 2, 3, 4, 5.

22

For stretching 2 and 4, and 4 and 5, and exercising 2, 3 and 4.

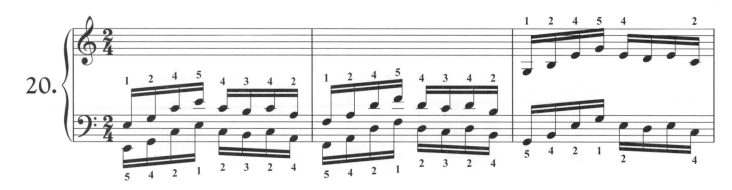

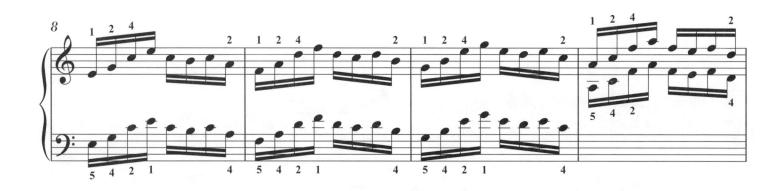

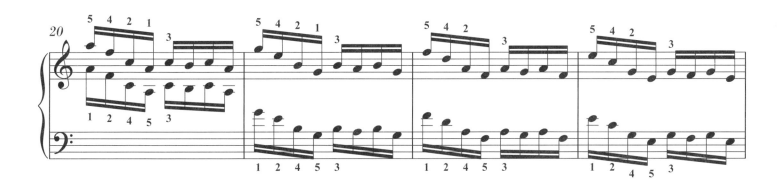

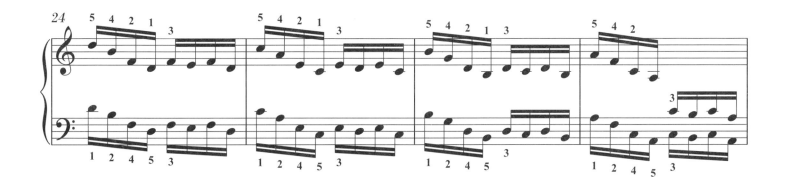

End of Part One

As soon as we have learned Part One, it will be played every day one or more times for a while, carefully avoiding any wrist tension before starting the study of the second transcendent part. With this new work, you will be certain to get from this book all the benefits it promises. By mastering this first part you will hold the key to the challenges of the second part.

THE VIRTUOSO PIANIST

PART TWO

*Transcendent Exercises for Preparing the
Fingers for the Viruoso Exercises*

Part Two

Charles Louis Hanon

Note that the work of the 3rd, 4th and 5th fingers of the left hand on the first beat of each measure is played in contrary motion by the same fingers of the right hand on the third beat of the same measure.

Once one has mastered this exercise, go on to play the next without stopping on the final note. The exercises of the second part are to be studied as were those of the first part, with the metronome at [quarter note] = 60 gradually increasing to [quarter note] = 108. Any of the following exercises without a fixed metronome indication should be played this way. When the tempo is different from this, it will be stated at the head of each such exercise.

The same aim as No. 21 (fingers 3, 4, 5).

We will study the exercises in Part Two as we have indicated for Part One at the head of exercise No. 3
(see the notes on this topic for that exercise). In Part Two stop only on the last note of exercises Nos. 22, 24,
26, 28, 30, 33, 35 and 38.

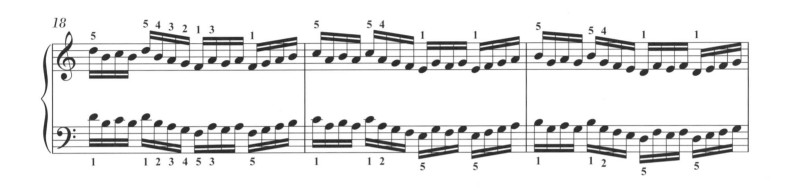

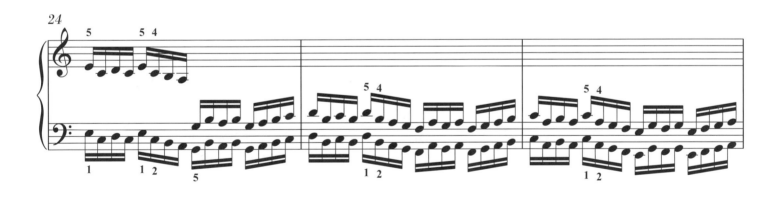

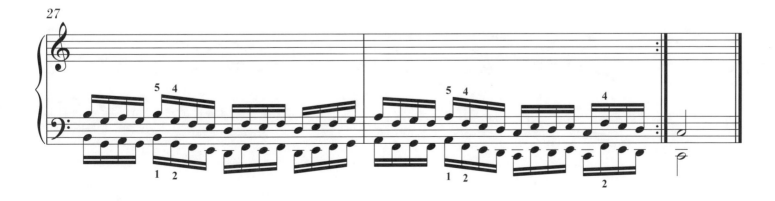

Fingers to be trained: 3, 4, 5.

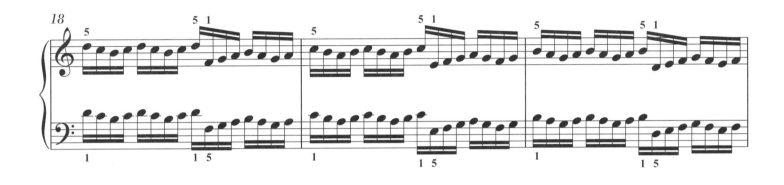

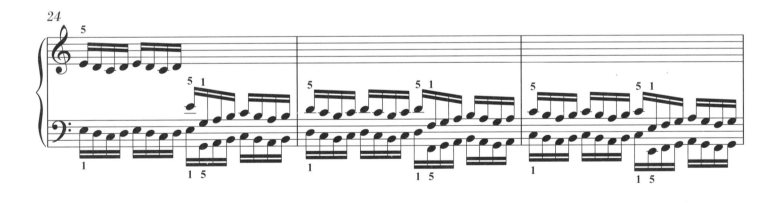

Fingers to be trained: 3, 4, 5.

34

Fingers to be trained: 1, 2, 3, 4, 5.

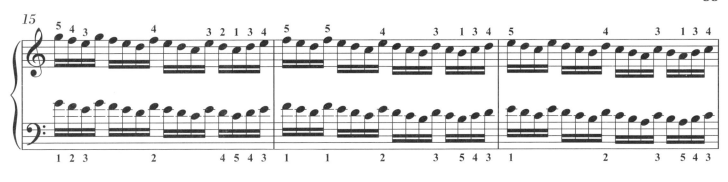

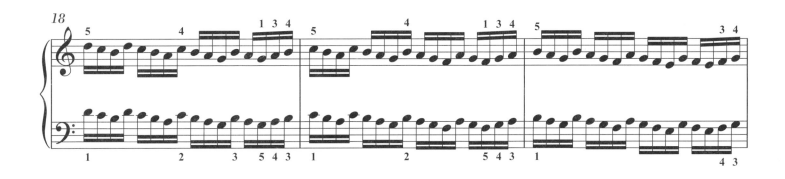

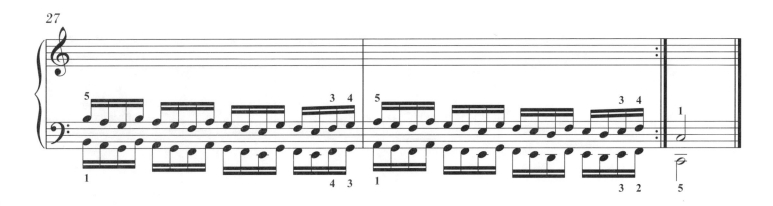

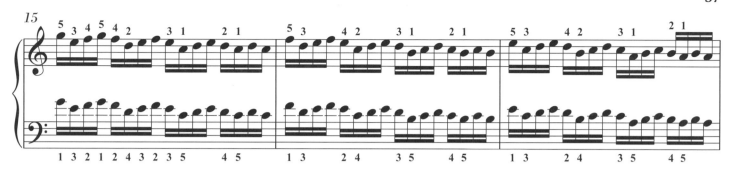

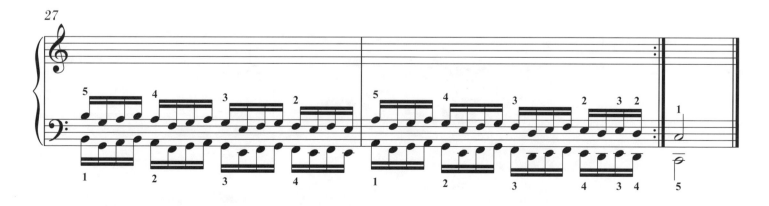

Fingers to be trained: 1, 2, 3, 4, 5. Preparing the 4th and 5th fingers for the trill which will be seen below.

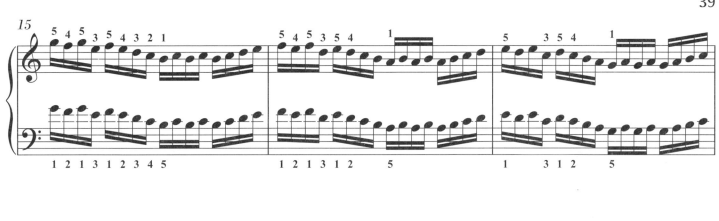

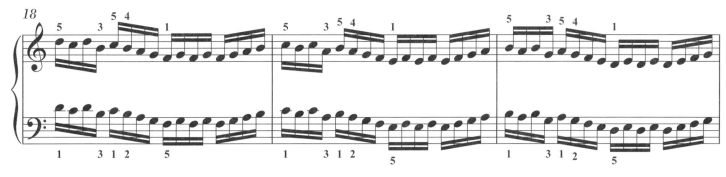

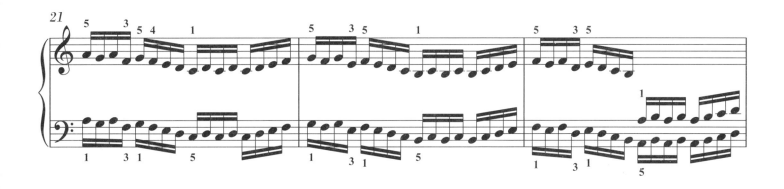

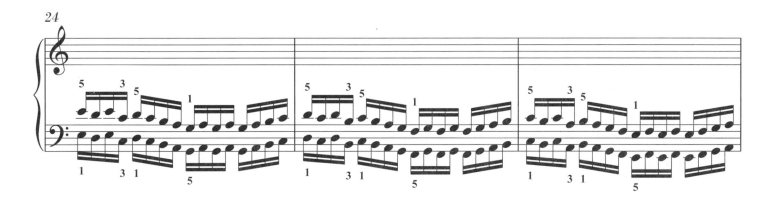

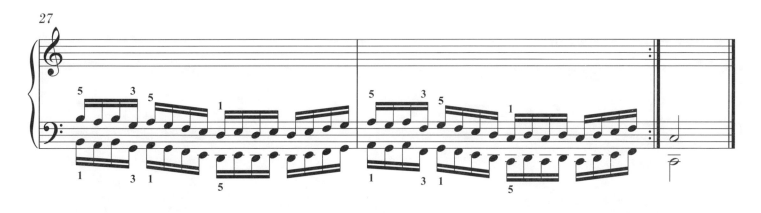

Fingers to be trained: 3, 4, 5.

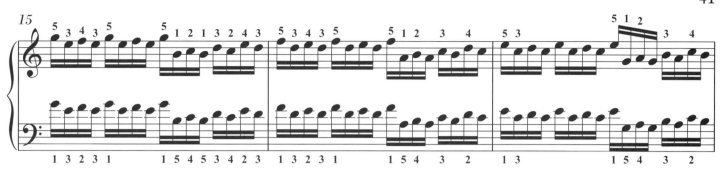

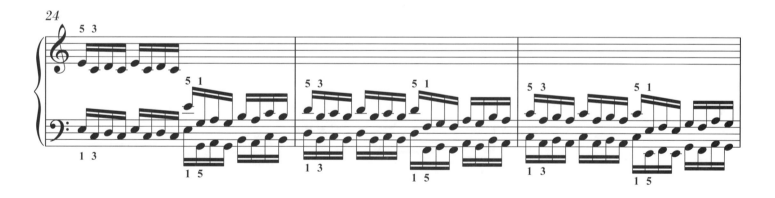

41

42

Fingers to be trained: 1, 2, 3, 4, 5. Preparation for the trill with the 5 fingers.

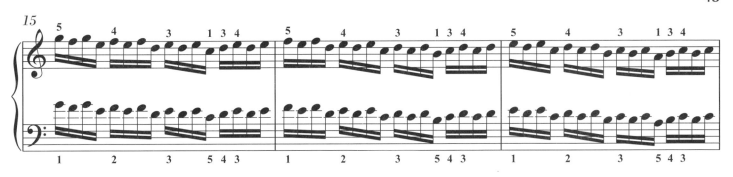

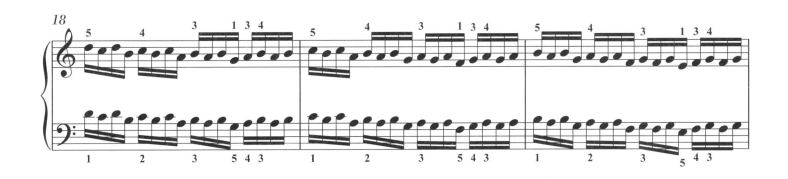

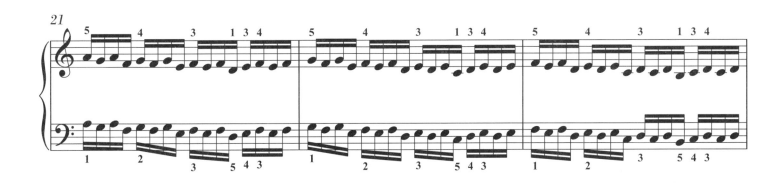

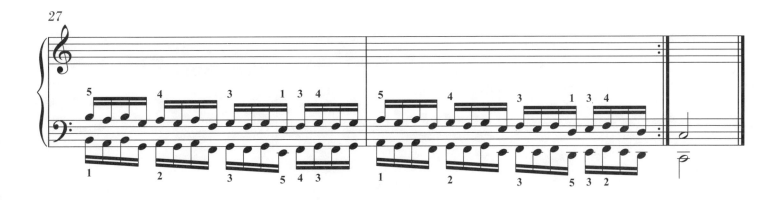

Alternate trill for the 1st and 2nd fingers, and the 4th and 5th fingers.

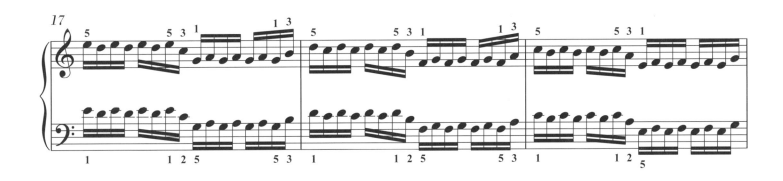

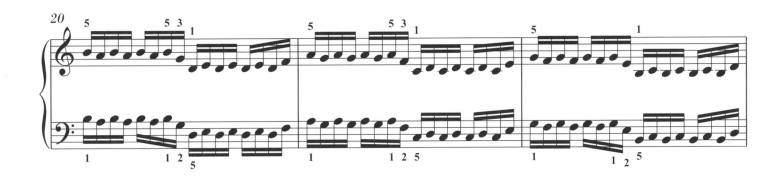

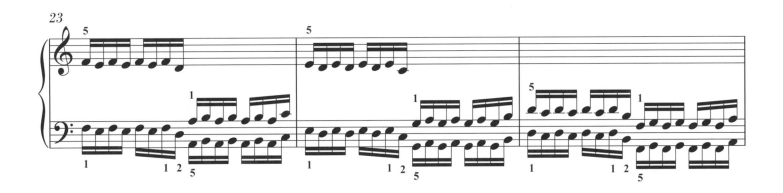

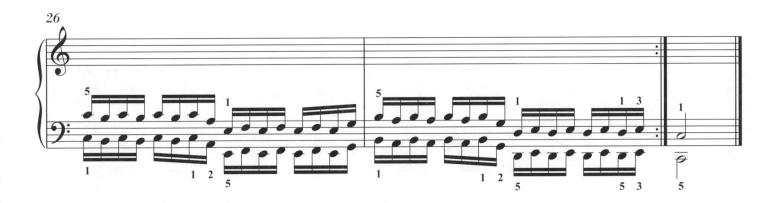

46

For exercising and stretching the five fingers.

Passing the thumb under the 2nd finger. Play the first bar 4 times.

M.M. ♩ = 40, progressively increasing to 72

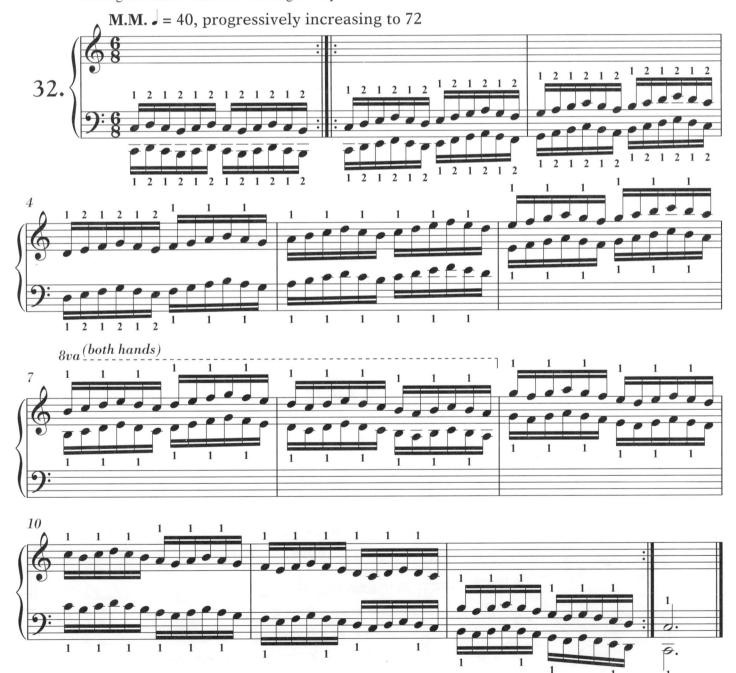

48

Passing the thumb under the 3rd finger. Play the first bar 4 times.

M.M. ♩ = 40, progressively increasing to 72

33.

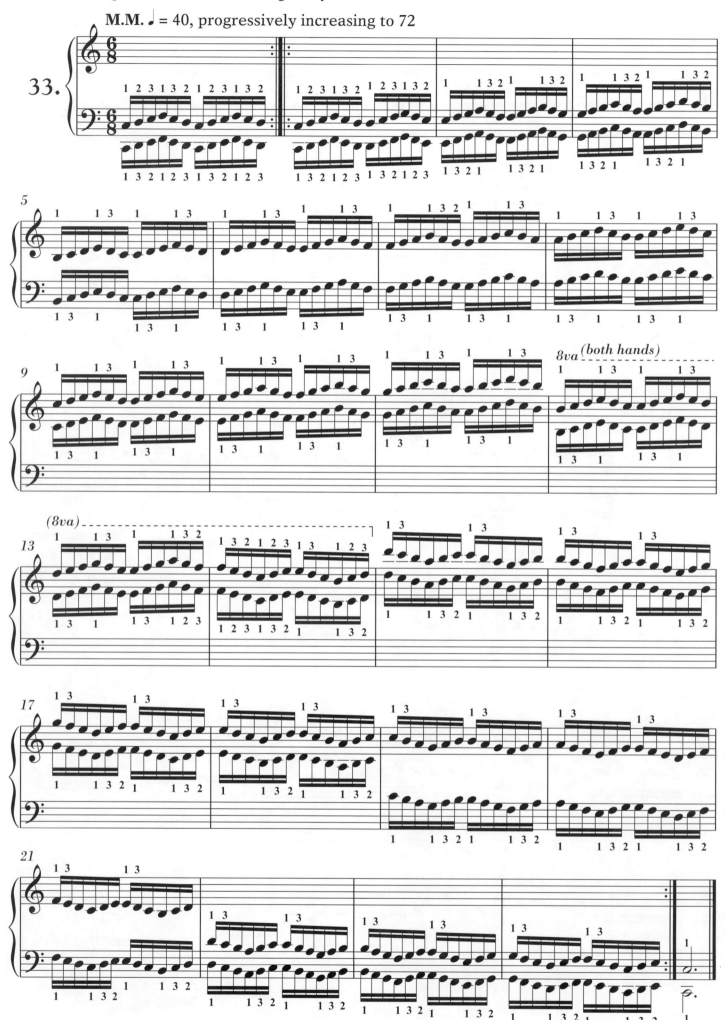

Passing the thumb under the 4th finger. Play the first bar 10 times.

M.M. ♩ = 60, progressively increasing to 108

34.

50

Passing the thumb under the 5th finger. Play the first bar 10 times.

M.M. ♩ = 40, progressively increasing to 72

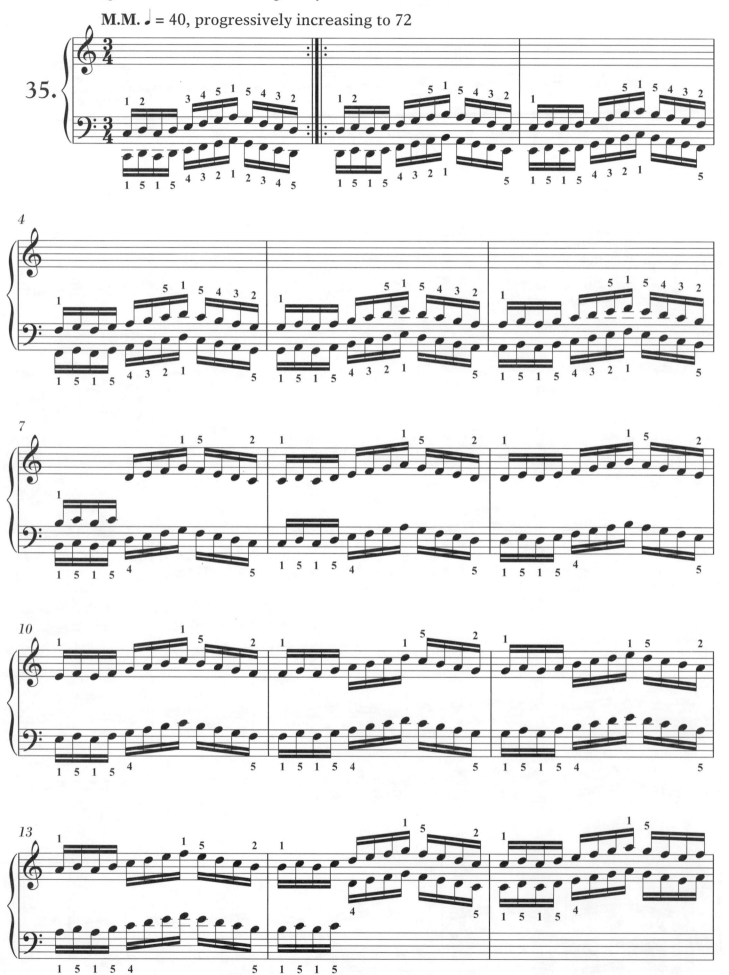

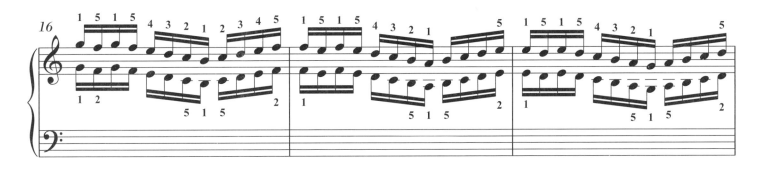

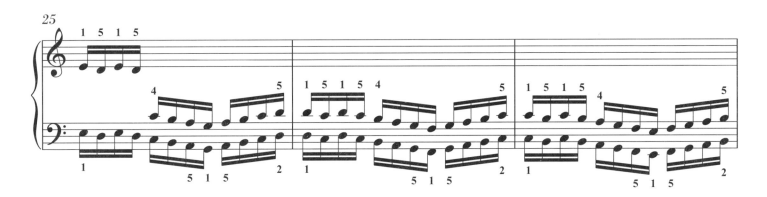

Another example of passing the thumb.

Passing the Thumb. Special Exercise. The whole of this exercise is to be played with the two thumbs only.

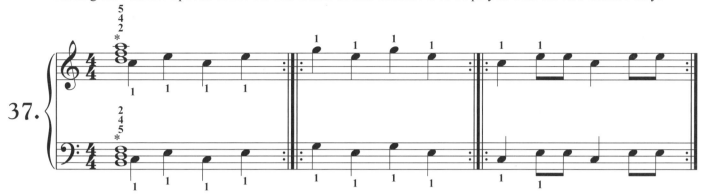

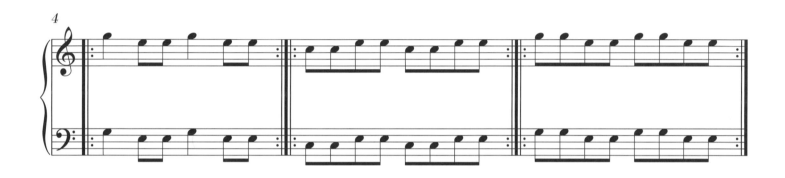

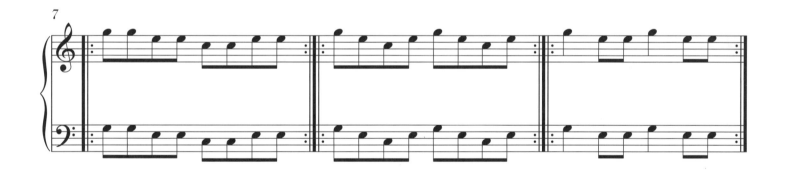

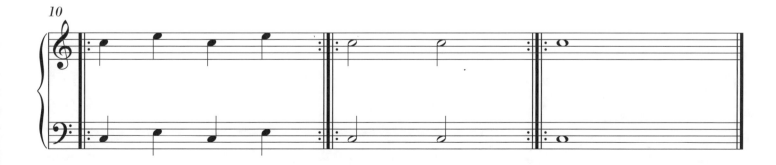

*Silently hold down these three chord notes without striking them while these 12 measures are played.

Exercise for preparing to study the scales.

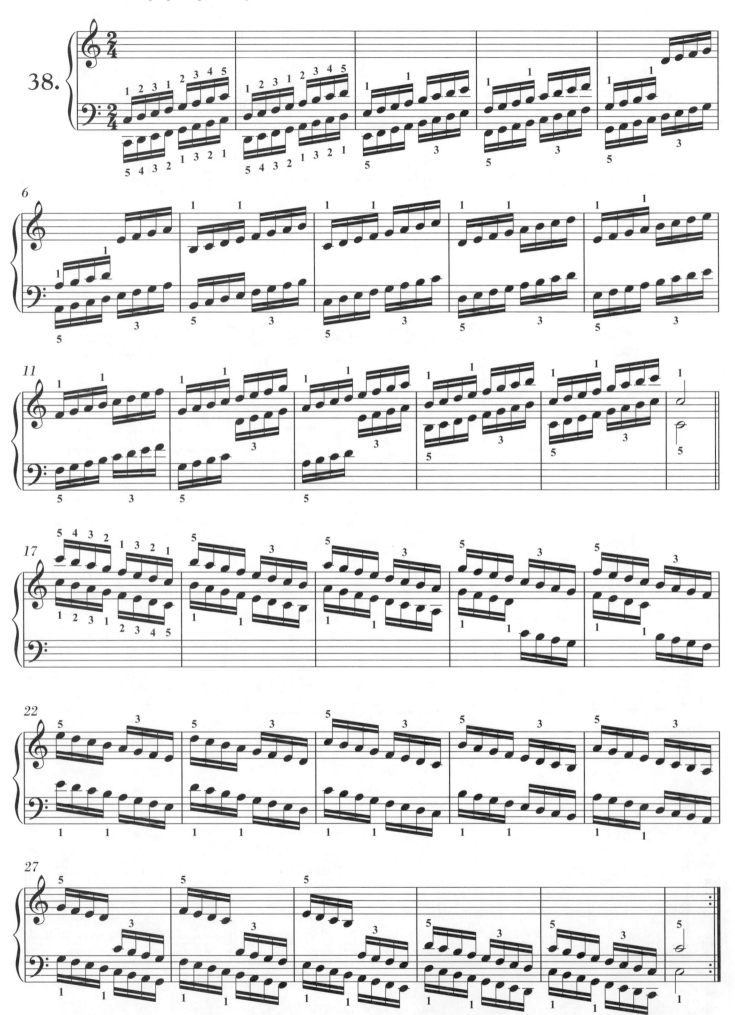

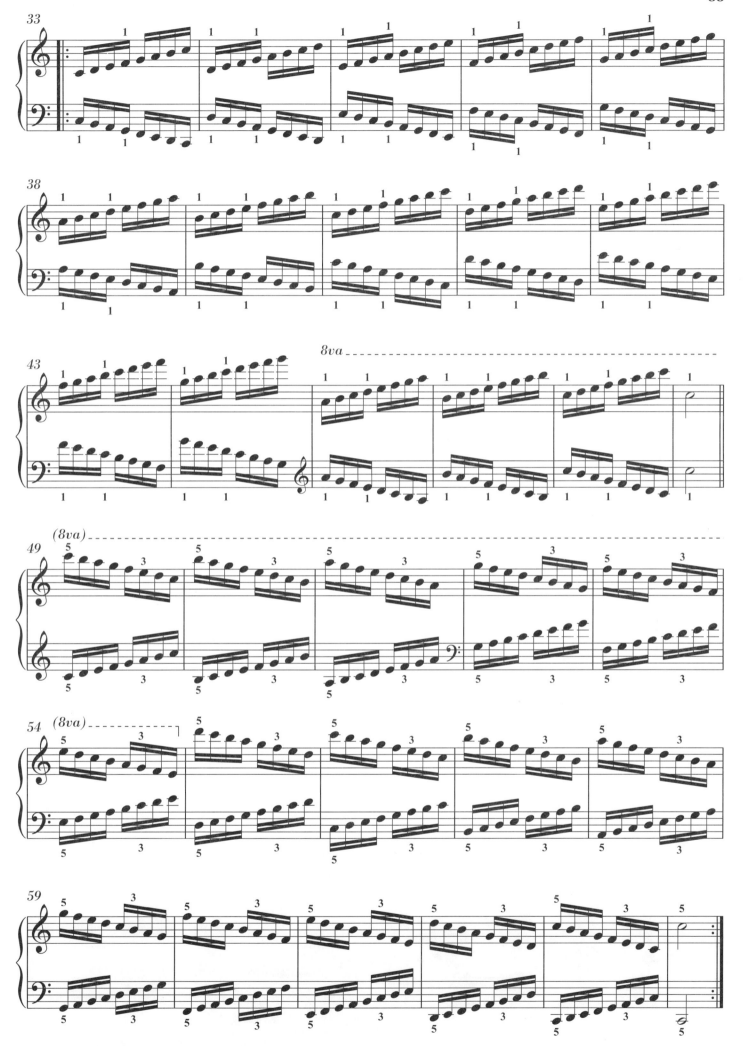

The 12 Major Scales, and the 12 Minor Scales
Each major scale is followed by its relative minor

There are two ways of playing the minor scale; we thought it best to give them here after each major scale, leaving it to the instructor to teach them as he [sic.] sees fit. We mark by a figure 1 the first (modern) minor scale, also termed the "harmonic minor scale"; and by a figure 2 the second (ancient) minor scale, also termed the "melodic minor scale."

We know that the modern or harmonic minor scale has a minor sixth and the leading-note both ascending and descending; whereas the ancient or melodic minor scale has a major sixth and the leading note is ascending, and a minor seventh and minor sixth in descending.

B-flat major

1. G minor

2. G minor

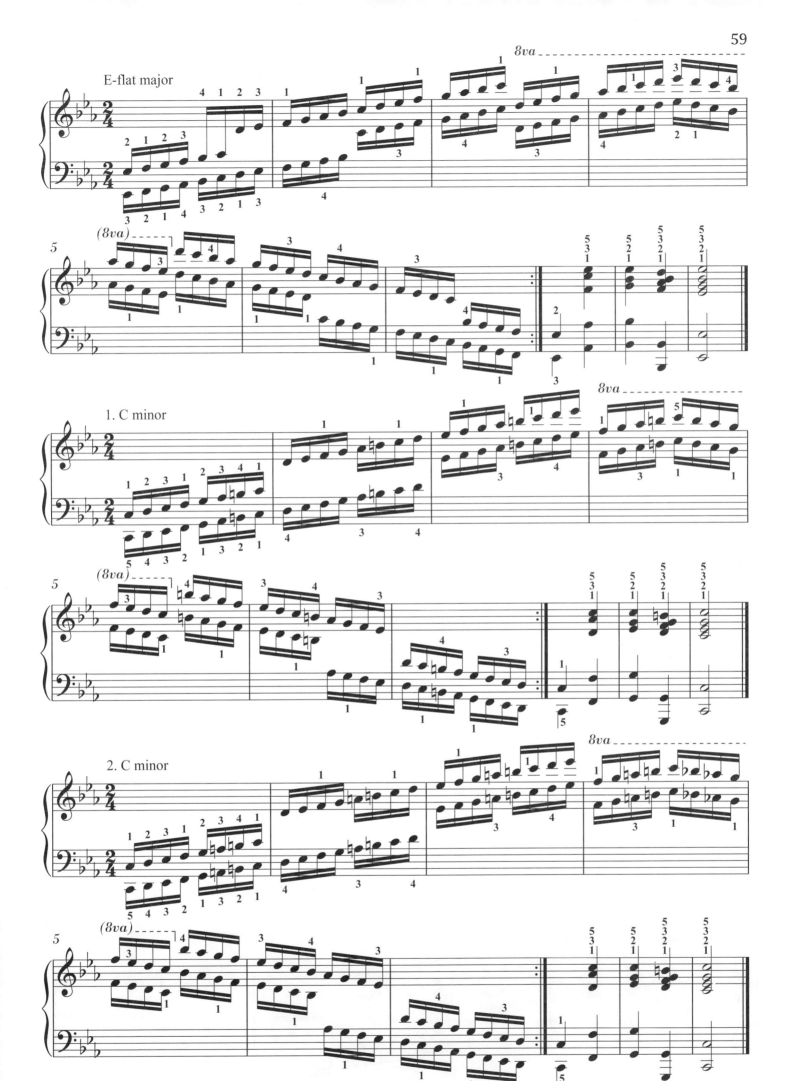

60

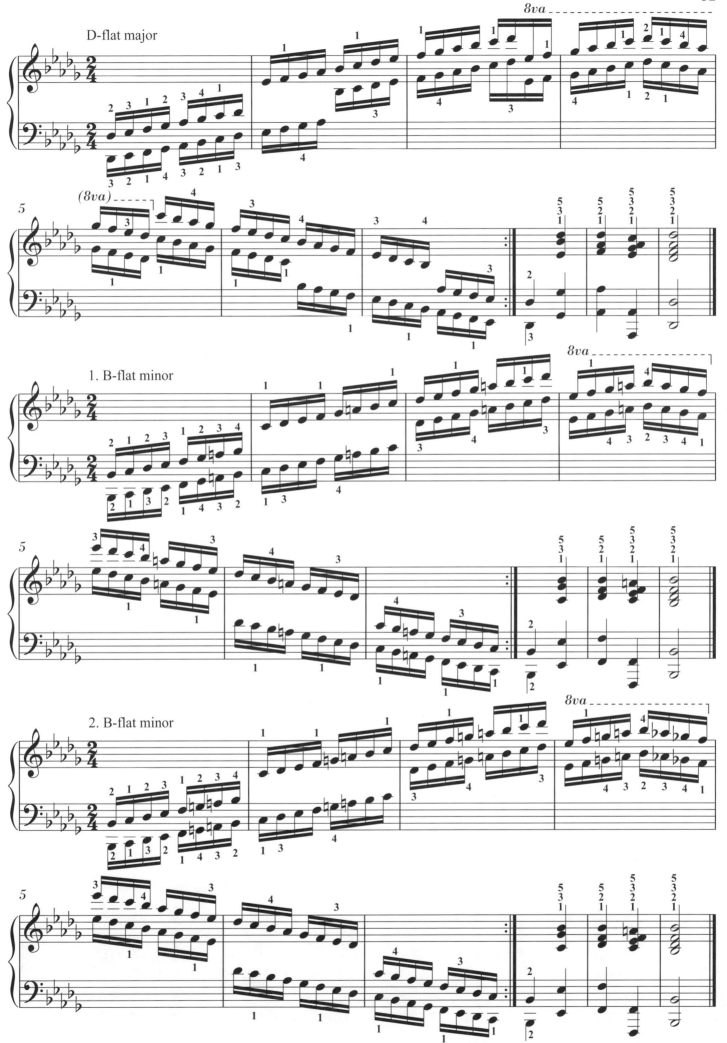

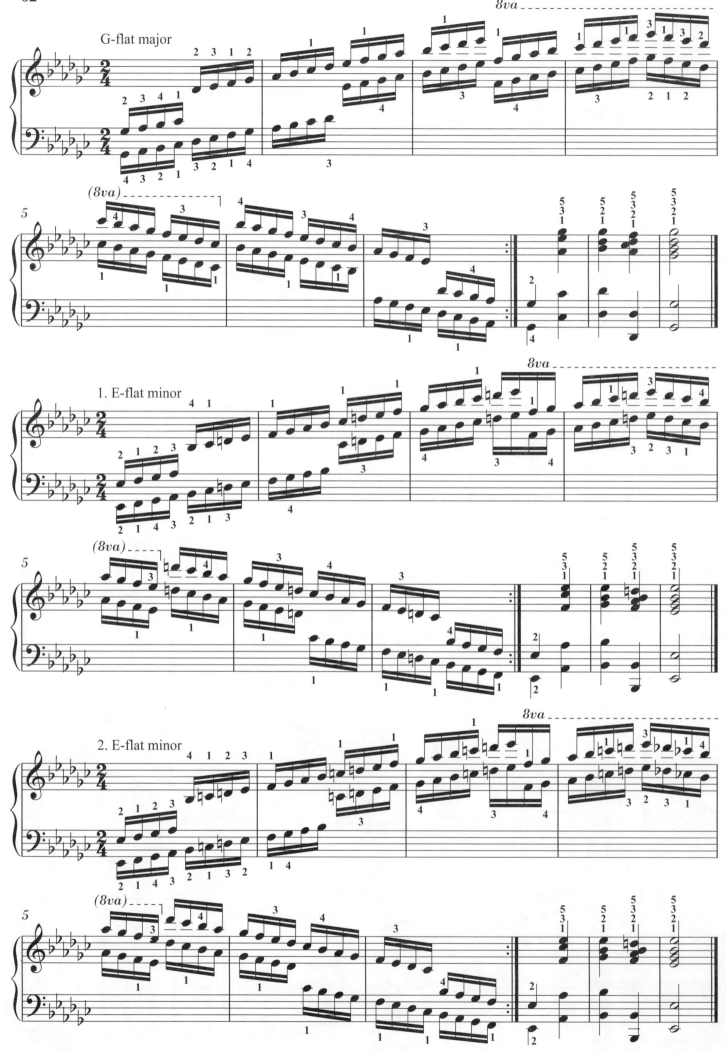

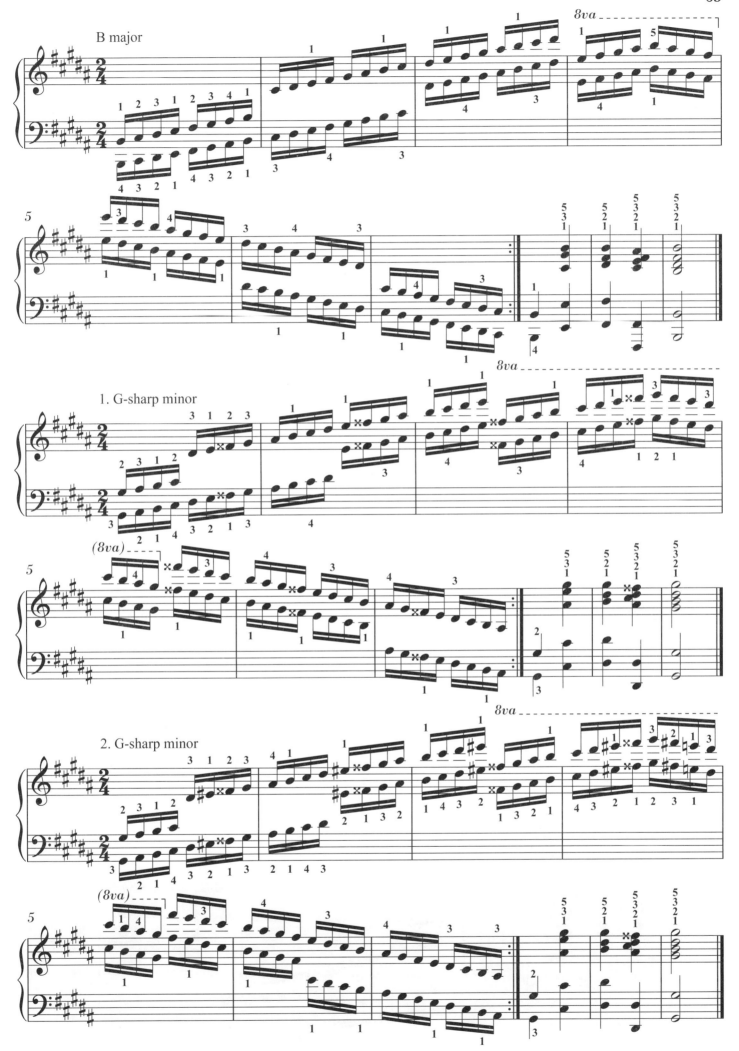

68

Chromatic Scales

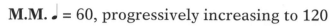

*Same fingering in playing the scale in major thirds.

In Major Sixths

In Minor Sixths

In contrary motion, beginning on the octave

In contrary motion, beginning on the minor third

In contrary motion, beginning on the major third

Fingering for the related passages

Arpeggios on the Triads, in the 24 Keys

M.M. ♩ = 60, progressively increasing to 108

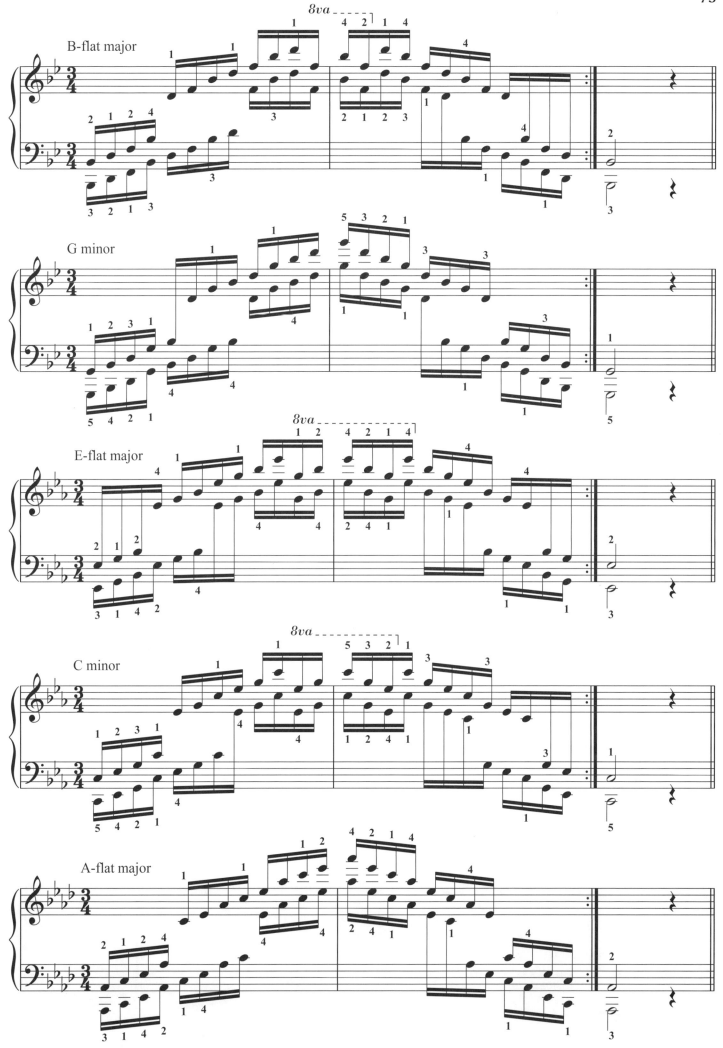

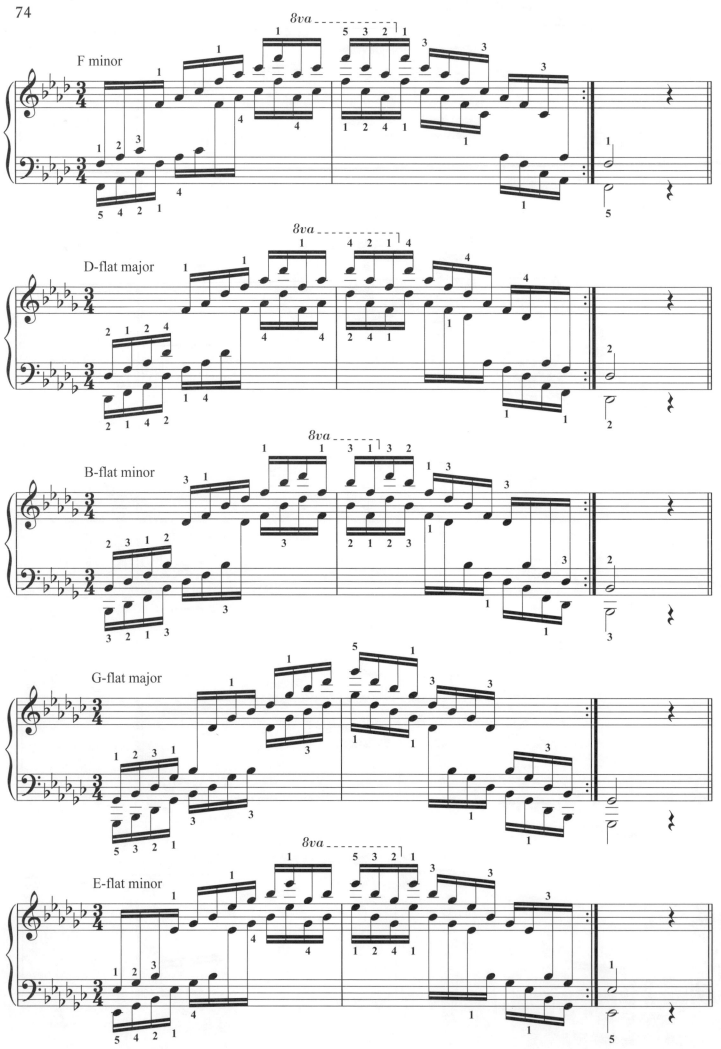

76

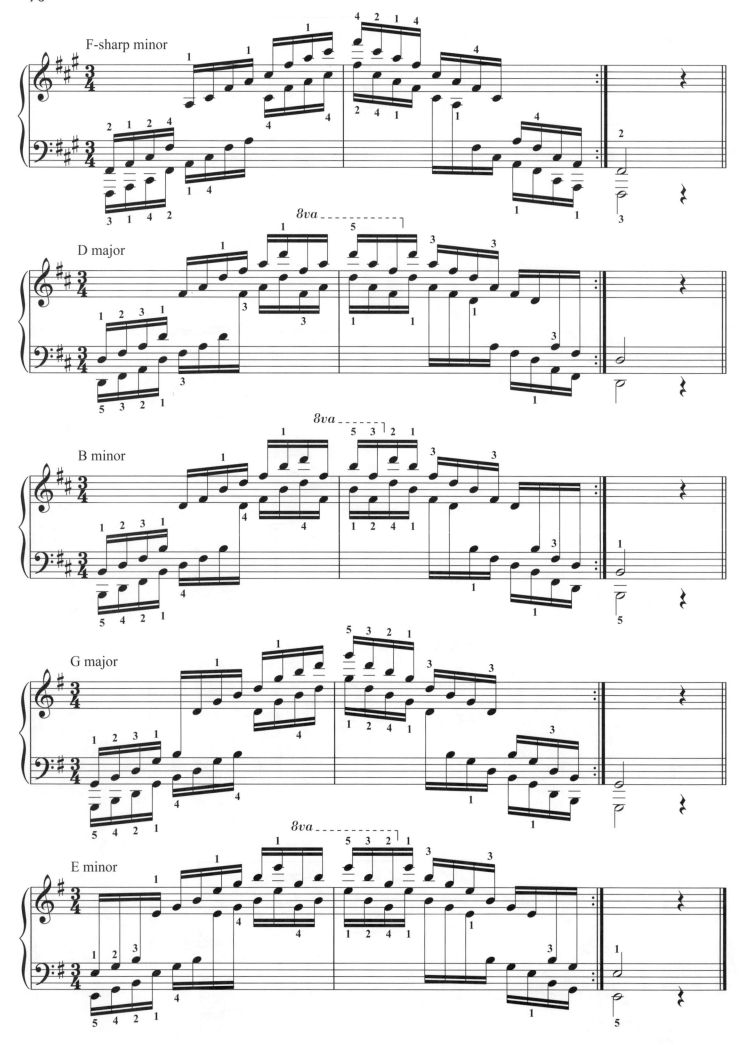

Finger stretching with selected diminished seventh chords in arpeggios.

M.M. ♩ = 60, progressively increasing to 120

*Play four times.

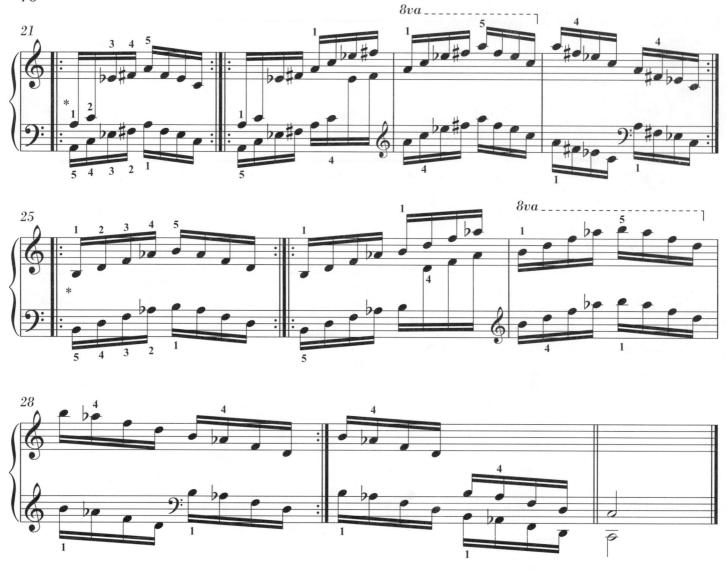

Finger stretching with selected dominant seventh chords in arpeggios.

M.M. ♩ = 60, progressively increasing to 120

*Play four times.

End of Part Two

Parts One and Two should be thoroughly mastered before attempting the virtuoso studies contained in Part Three.

THE VIRTUOSO PIANIST

PART THREE

Virtuoso Exercises, for Obtaining a Mastery
over the Greatest Mechanical Difficulties

Part Three

Charles Louis Hanon

Repeated notes by three. Play with well articulated fingers and a loose, free wrist.
When the first four bars have been mastered, move on to the rest of the exercise.

M.M. ♩ = 60, progressively increasing to 120

84

Repeated notes (by the five fingers and by two). Practice the first line until it can be played very well. Practice each of the following lines similarly. Then play the entire exercise without stopping if possible. Stop at the slightest sign of fatigue. The first of the two slurred notes is to be accented.

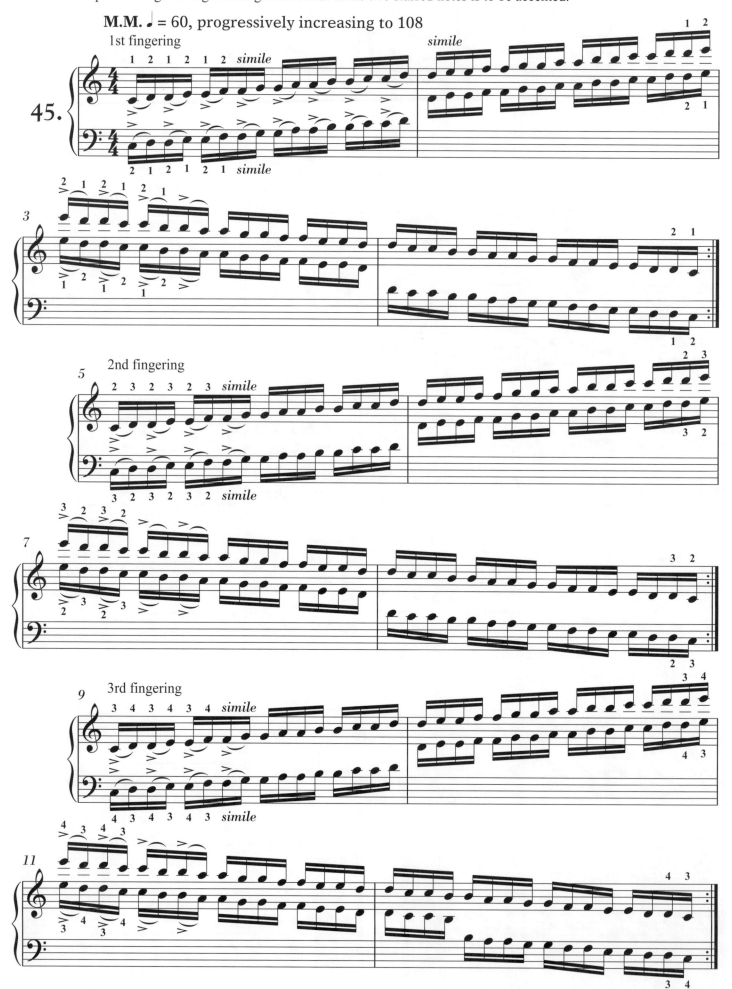

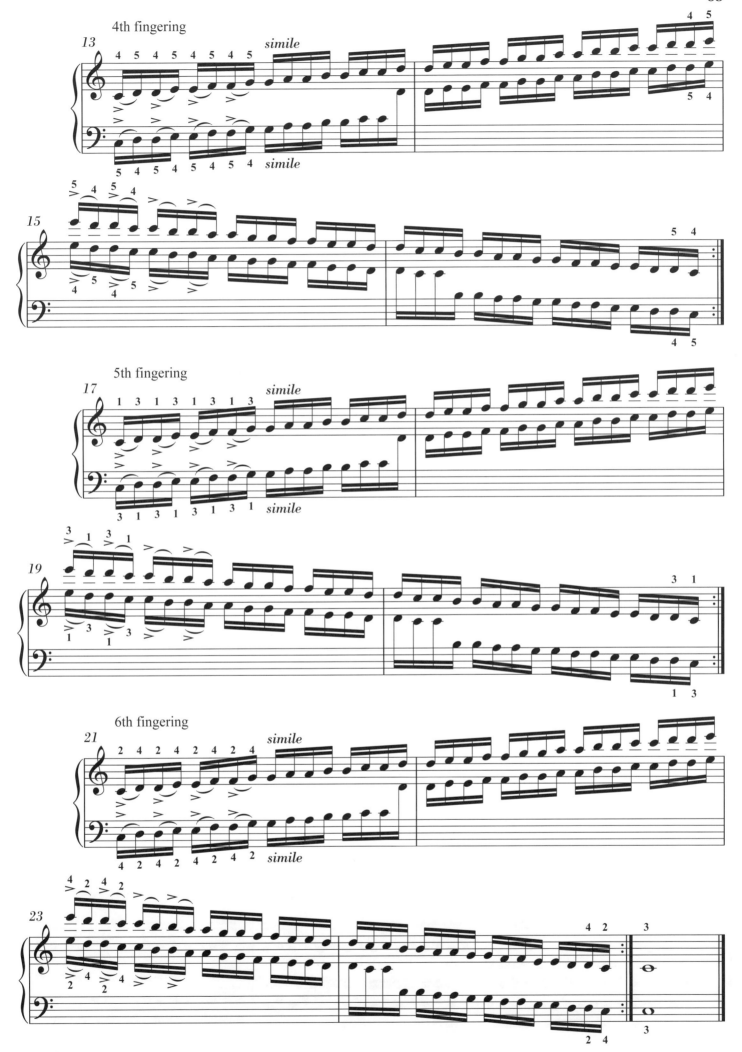

The trill for the five fingers. Practice the first line until it can be played quite rapidly,
then practice the rest of the trill. You must play with perfect equality the change over fingering.

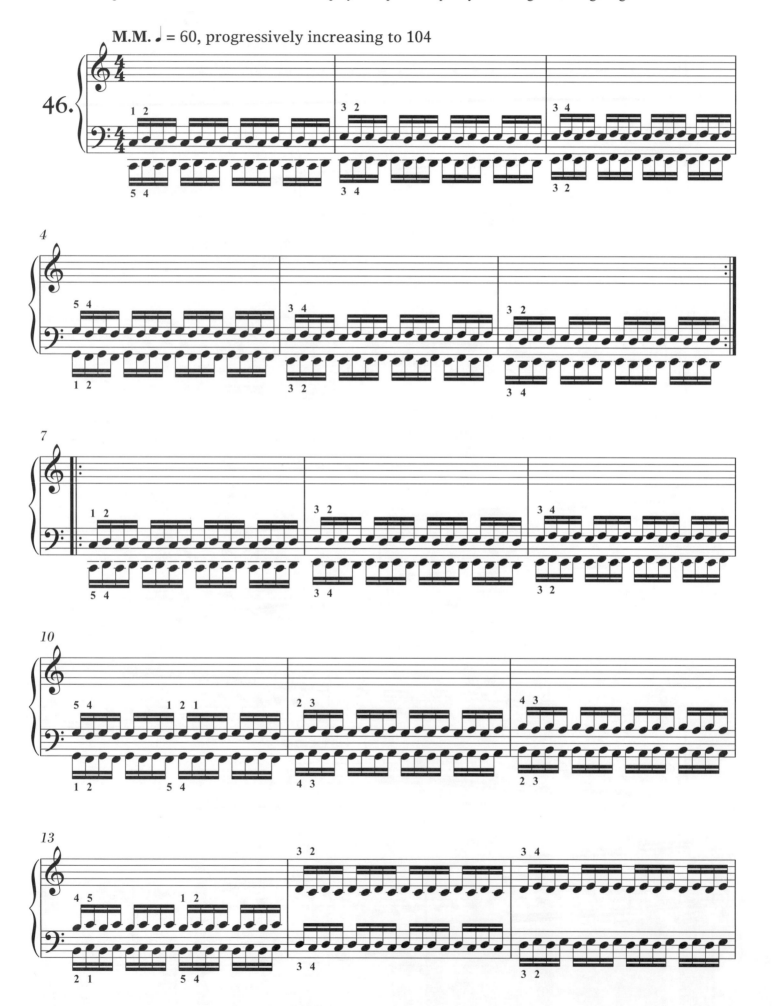

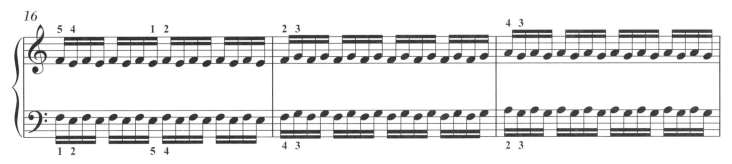

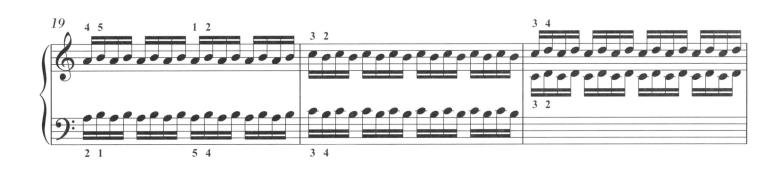

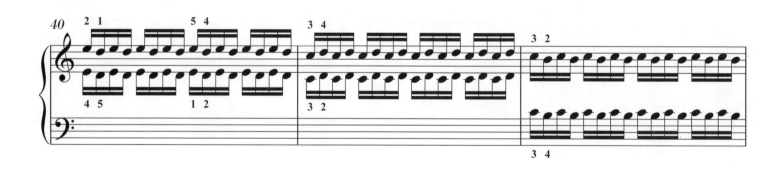

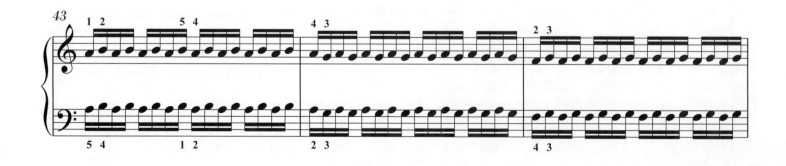

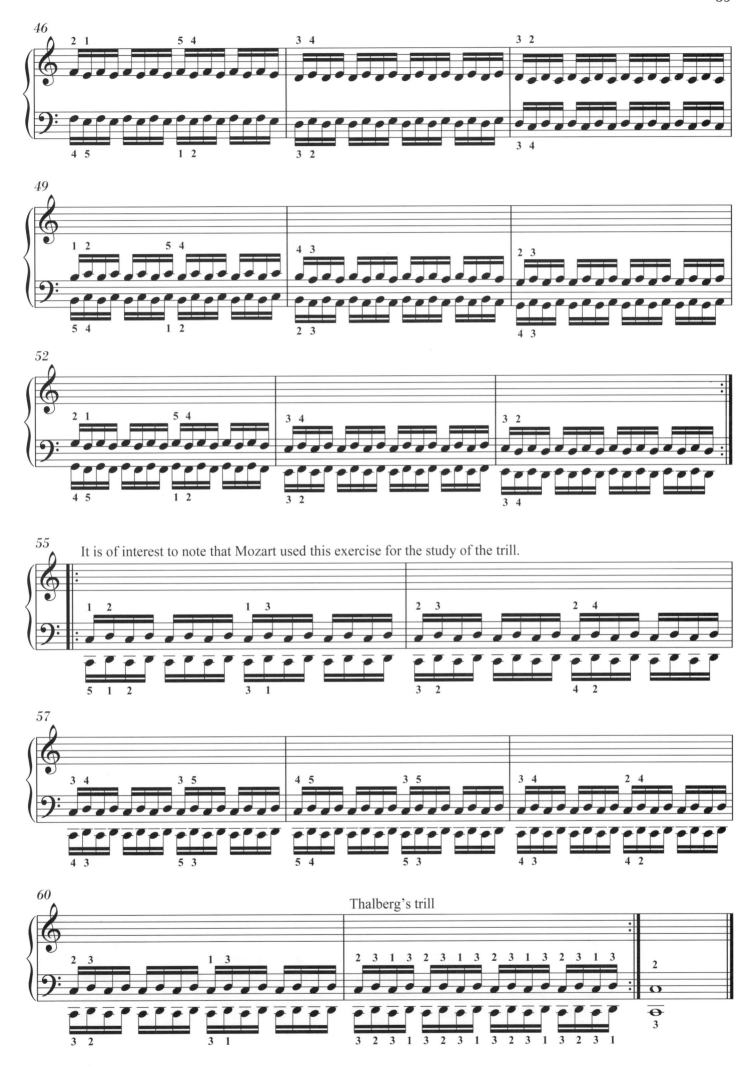

It is of interest to note that Mozart used this exercise for the study of the trill.

Thalberg's trill

90

Repeated notes by four. The fingers should articulate the fingers but not excessively throughout this exercise, always with flexibility in the wrist and arm. When the first four bars have been mastered, continue with the rest of the exercise.

M.M. ♩ = 60, progressively increasing to 120

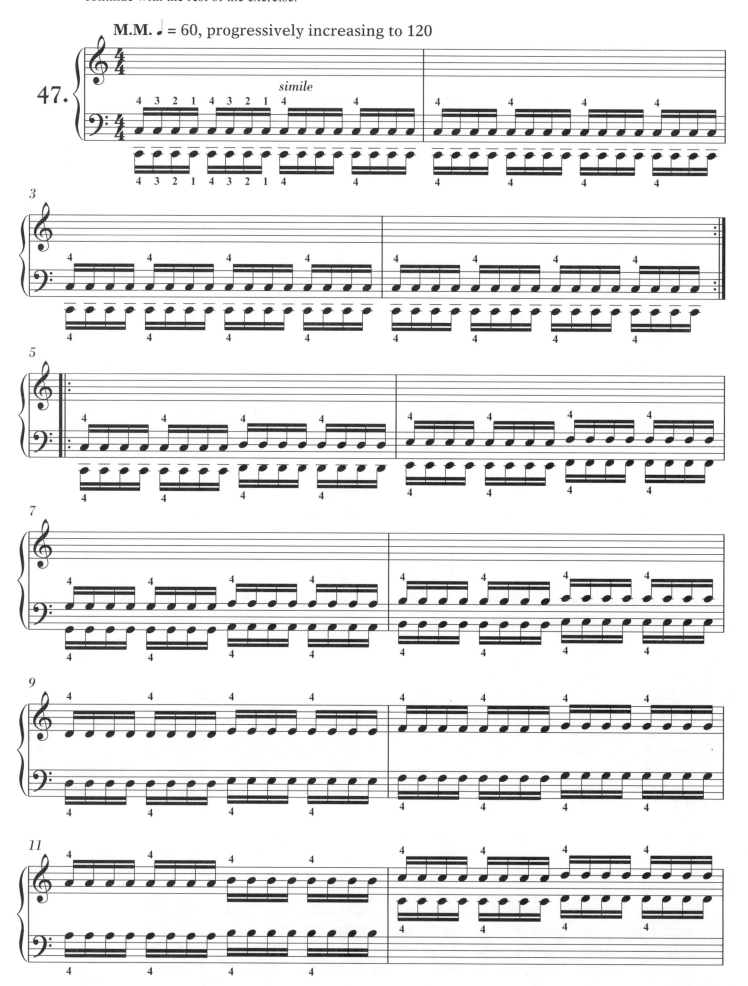

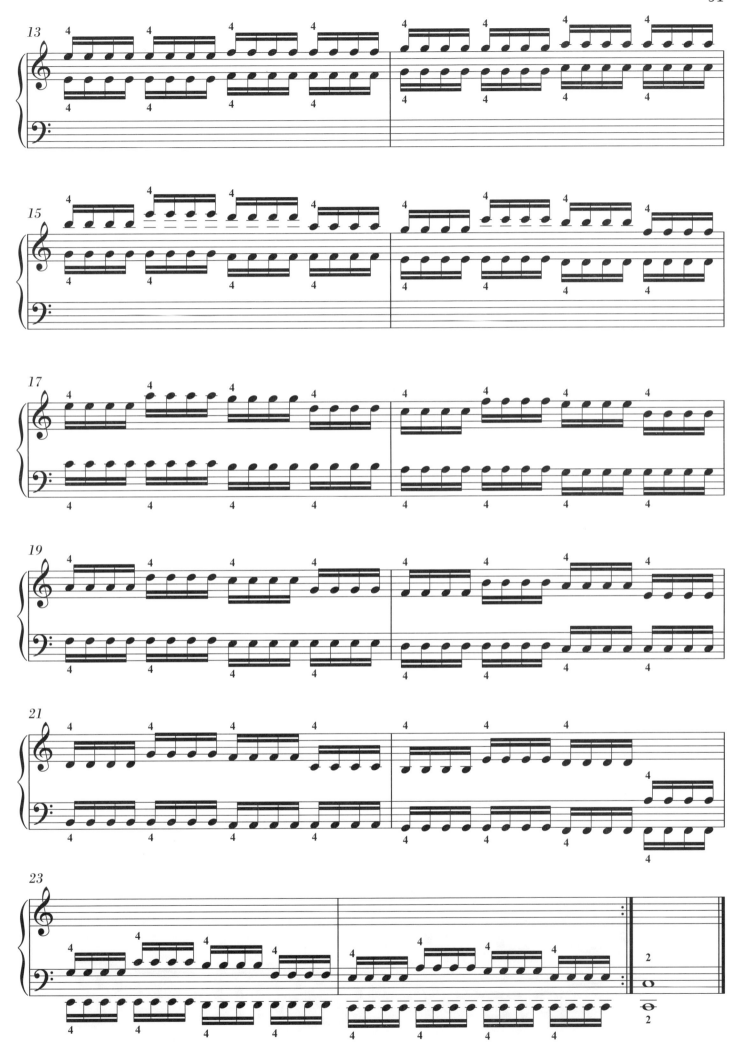

Although the wrists are to be well raised at each note, keep the arms very supple and the fingers firm but without stiffness. Play these four measures until easily articulated, then learn the rest of this exercise.

M.M. ♩ = 40, progressively increasing to 84

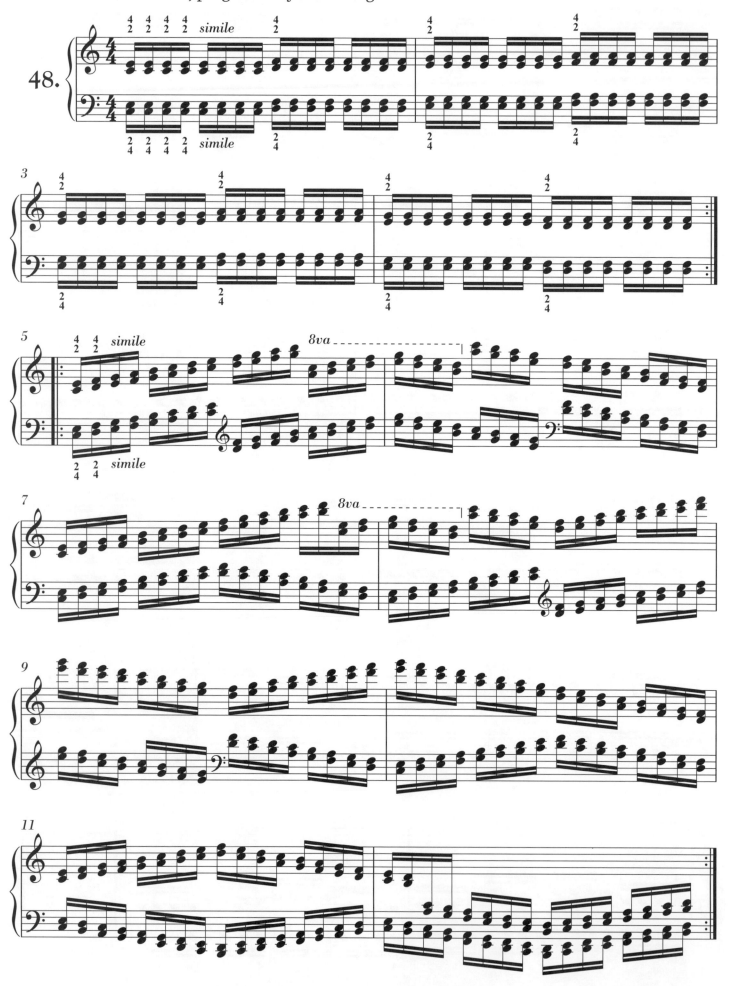

Detached sixths. Same remarks as for thirds.

M.M. ♩ = 40, progressively increasing to 84

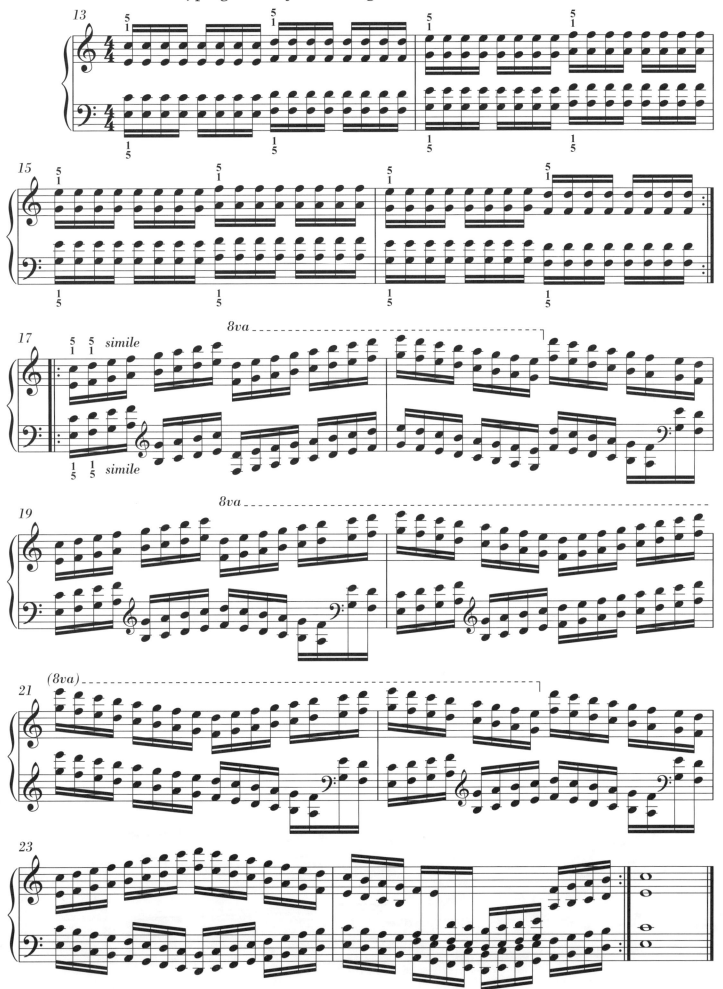

Sixths. Preparatory exercises. Stretching of the 1st to the 4th finger and the 2nd to the 5th finger of each hand. This exercise is very useful in facilitating the spreading of the fingers.

M.M. ♩ = 60, progressively increasing to 108

Continuation of the preceding exercise.

M.M. ♩ = 60, progressively increasing to 108

Double notes, thirds. We recommend practising this exercise in thirds thoroughly, as thirds are an important part in music for the piano. It is necessary that all the notes are played with equality and very distinctly.

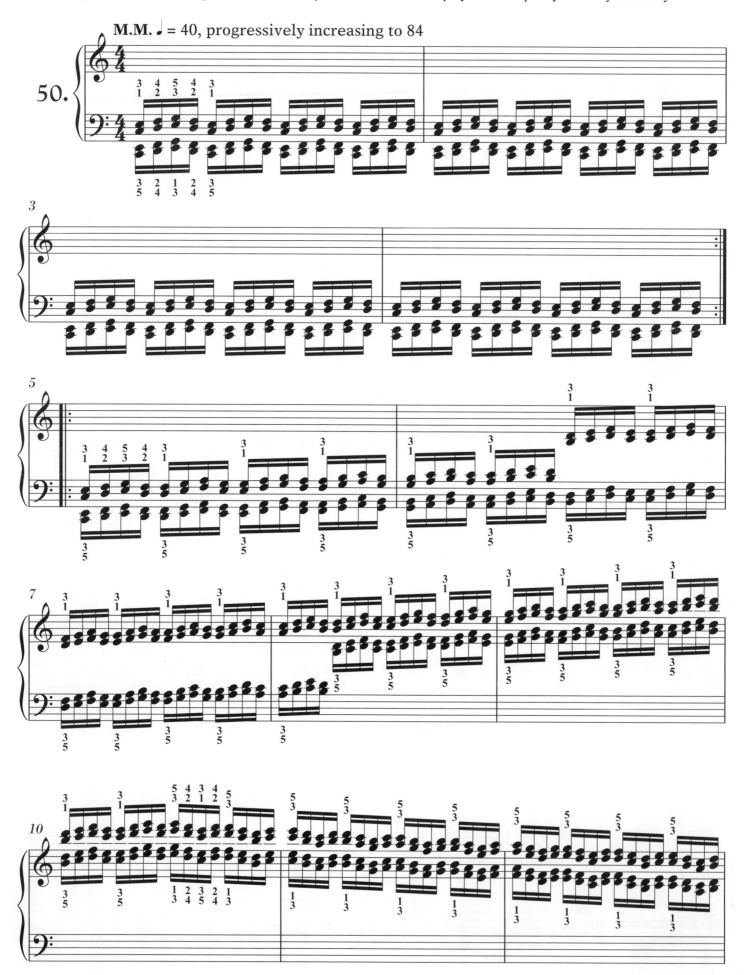

Scales in legato thirds. To obtain a smooth legato, keep the fifth finger of the right hand for an instant on its note while the thumb and 3rd finger are passing over to the next third. In the left hand, the thumb is similarly held for an instant. Notes to be held are indicated by half-notes. Proceed similarly in the chromatic scale further on, and in all scales in thirds.

M.M. ♩ = 40, progressively increasing to 84

Chromatic scales in minor thirds.

M.M. ♩ = 40, progressively increasing to 84

Preparatory exercises for playing the scales in octaves. The wrists should be very flexible as always, the fingers playing the octave must be firm but not stiff. The other three fingers should be slightly rounded. Repeat the first two lines slowly until it is easy to articulate the wrists, and then accelerate the tempo by continuing this exercise without interruption if possible. But if the wrists become fatigued, slow down or even stop until this fatigue is gone (see the notes after exercise No. 3).

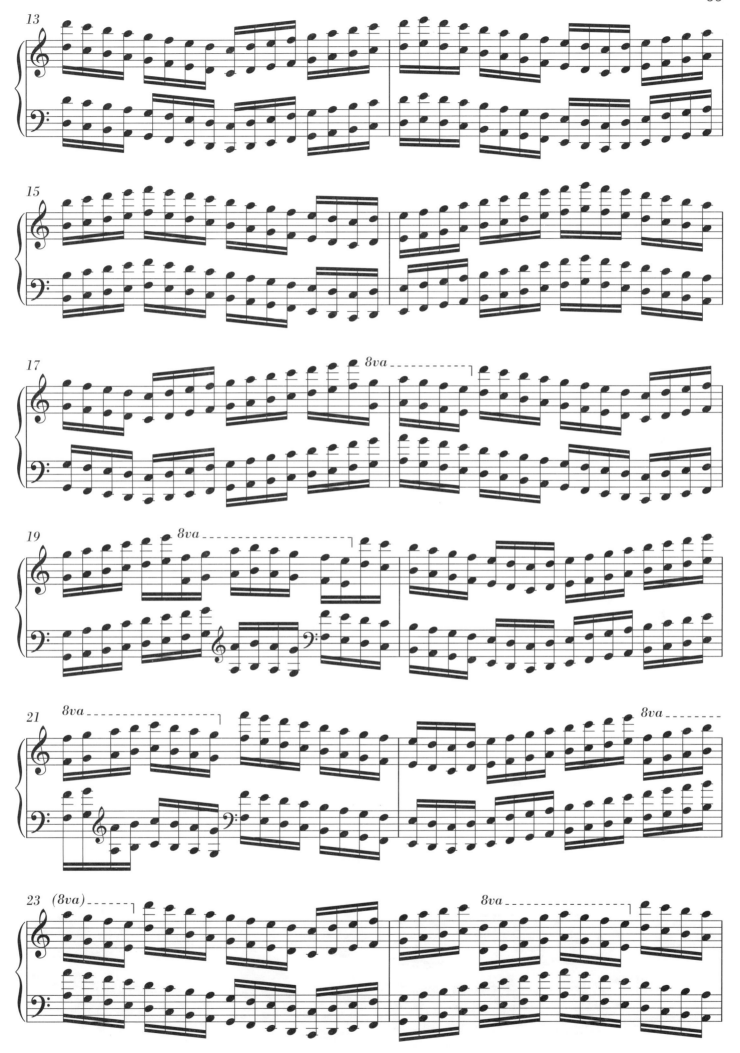

100

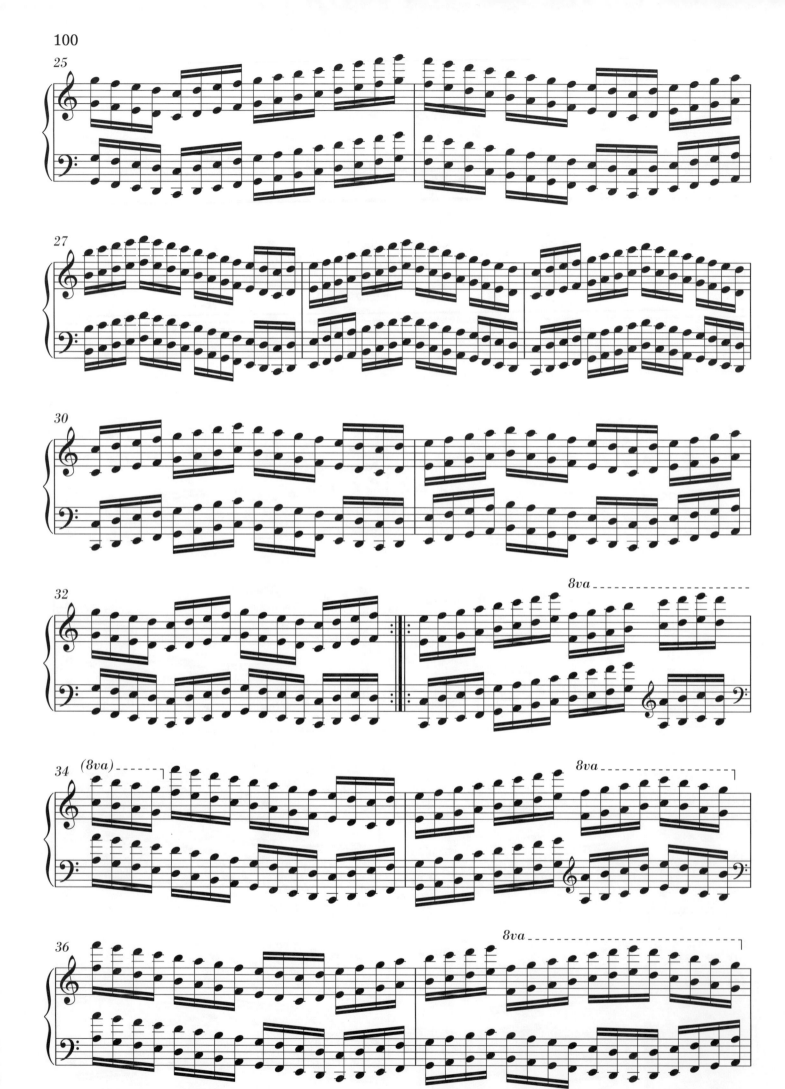

Scales in Thirds, in the keys most used. Play these scales legato, and very evenly; it is highly important to master them thoroughly. See remarks to No. 50.

M.M. ♩ = 40, progressively increasing to 84

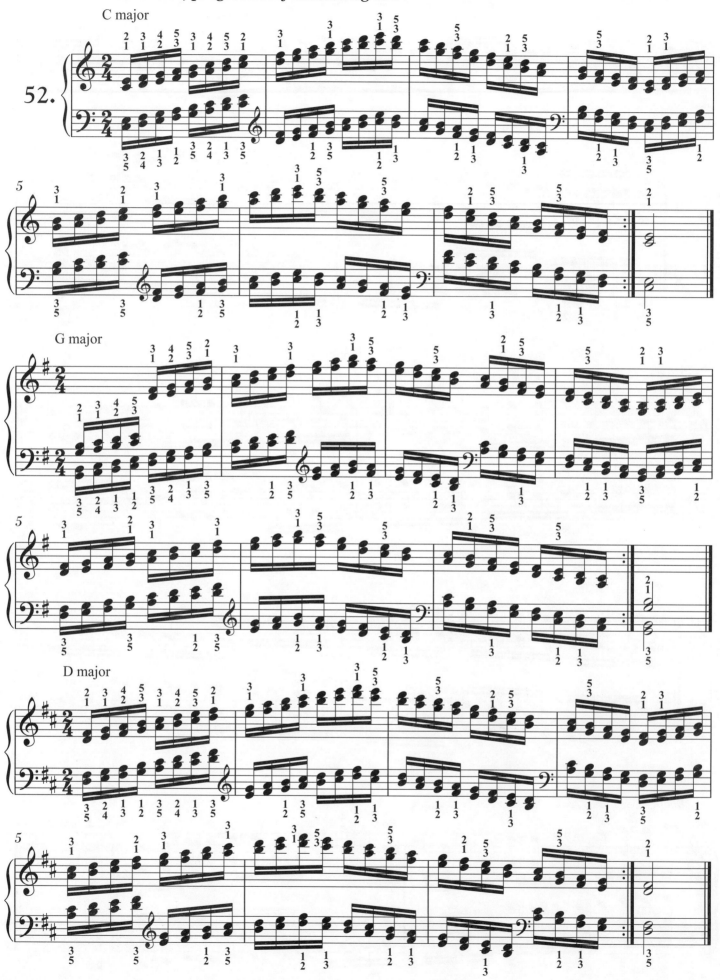

104

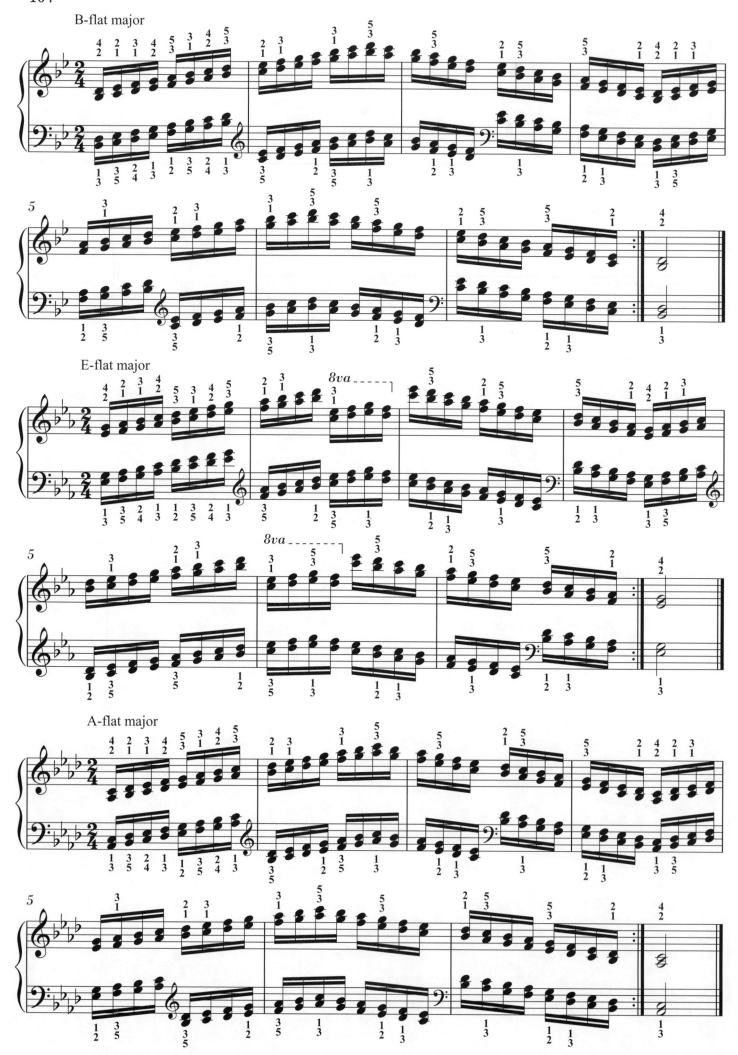

Octave Scales in the 24 Keys

First, practice each of these 24 scales until each scale can be played with ease; then play all 24 without interruption. However, it is always recommended to stop at any sign of fatigue. We cannot stress enough the absolute necessity of articulating the wrists. This is the only way to play octaves without stiffness, with flexibility, liveliness and energy.

M.M. ♩ = 40, progressively increasing to 84

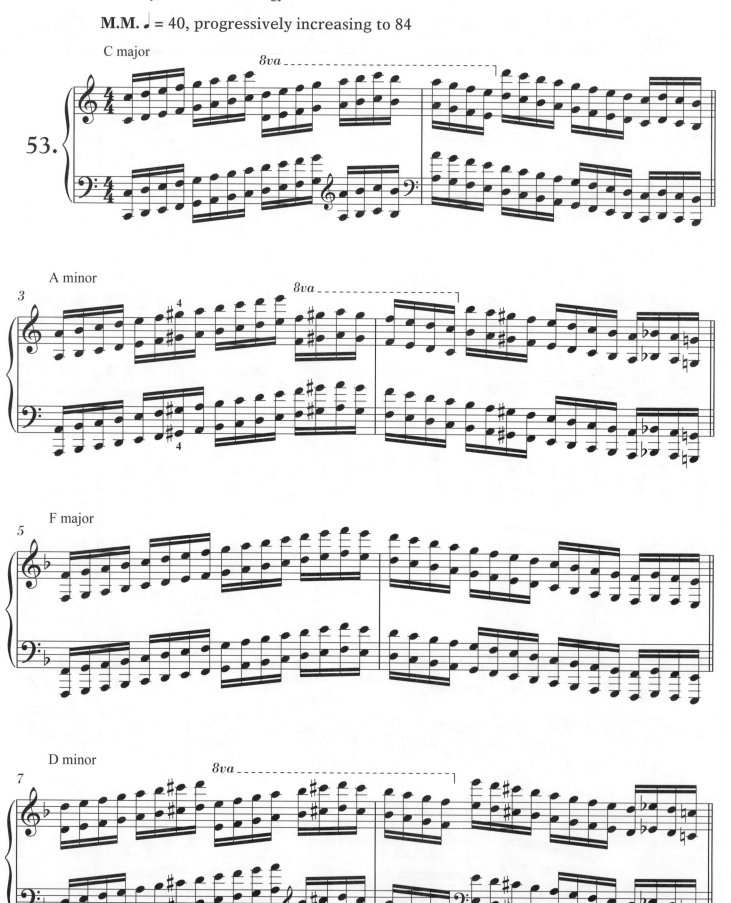

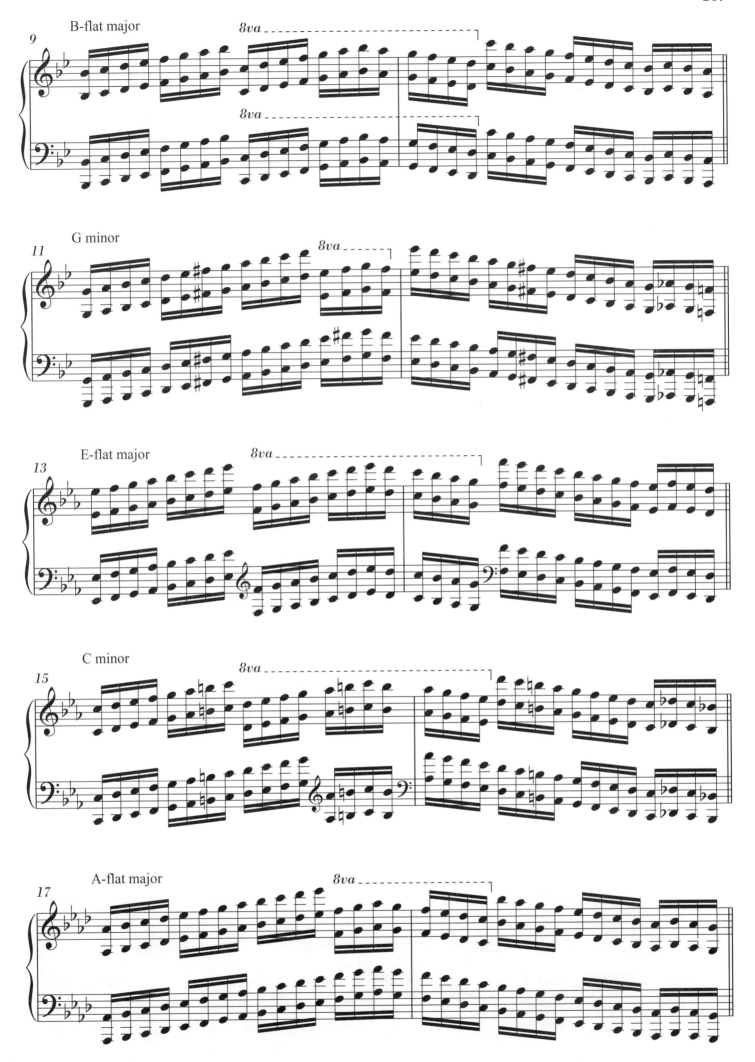

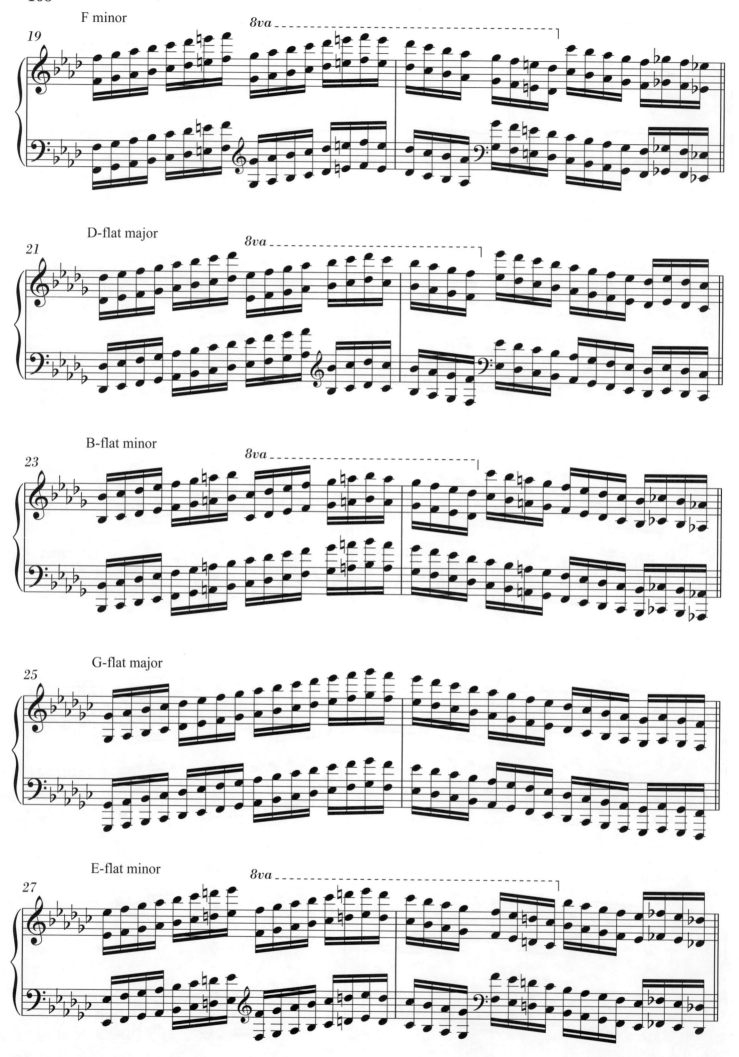

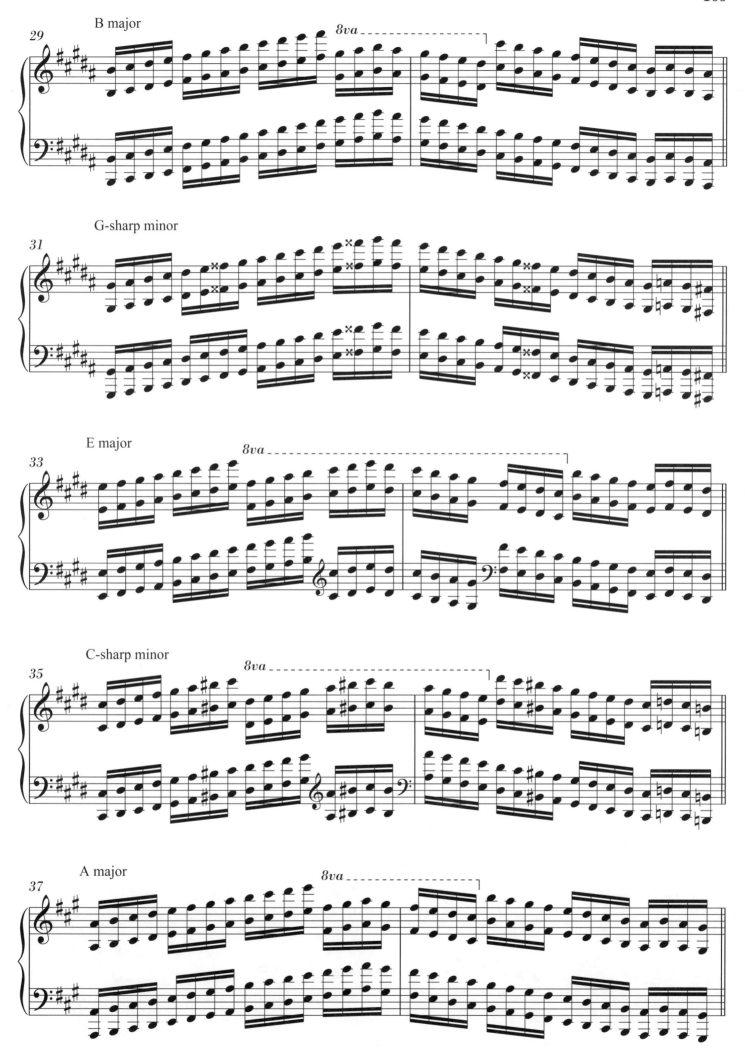

F-sharp minor

39

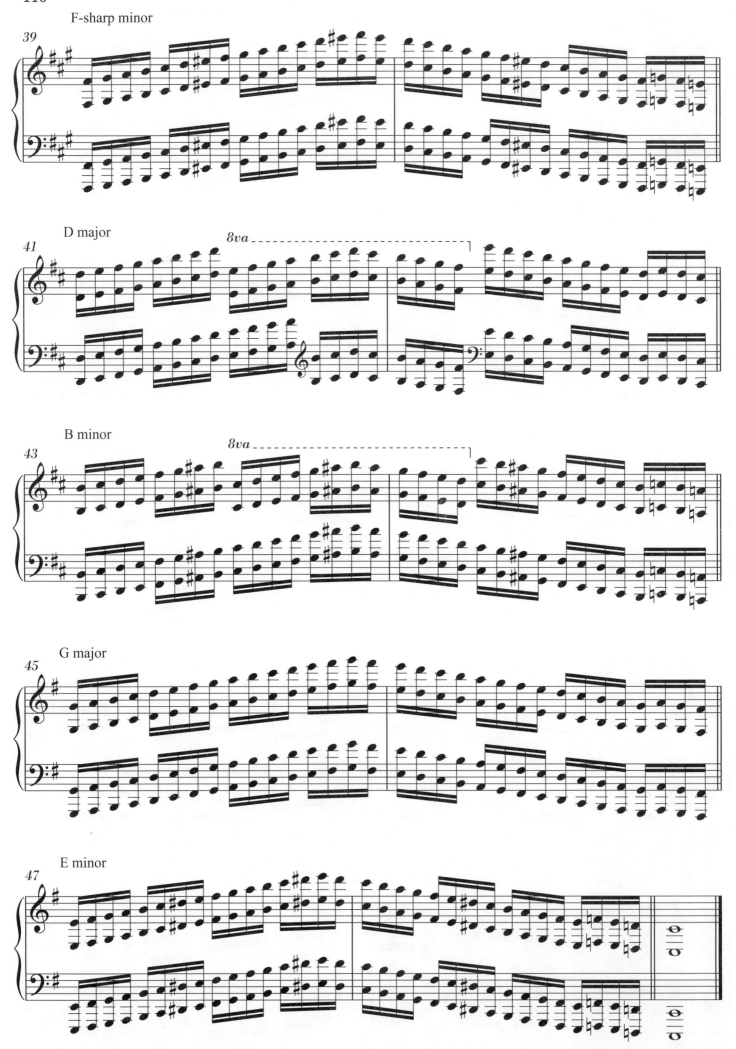

D major

41

B minor

43

G major

45

E minor

47

Quadruple trill in thirds for the five fingers. One must play this exercise with absolute equality, with each third being heard very distinctly.

M.M. ♩ = 40, progressively increasing to 92

54.

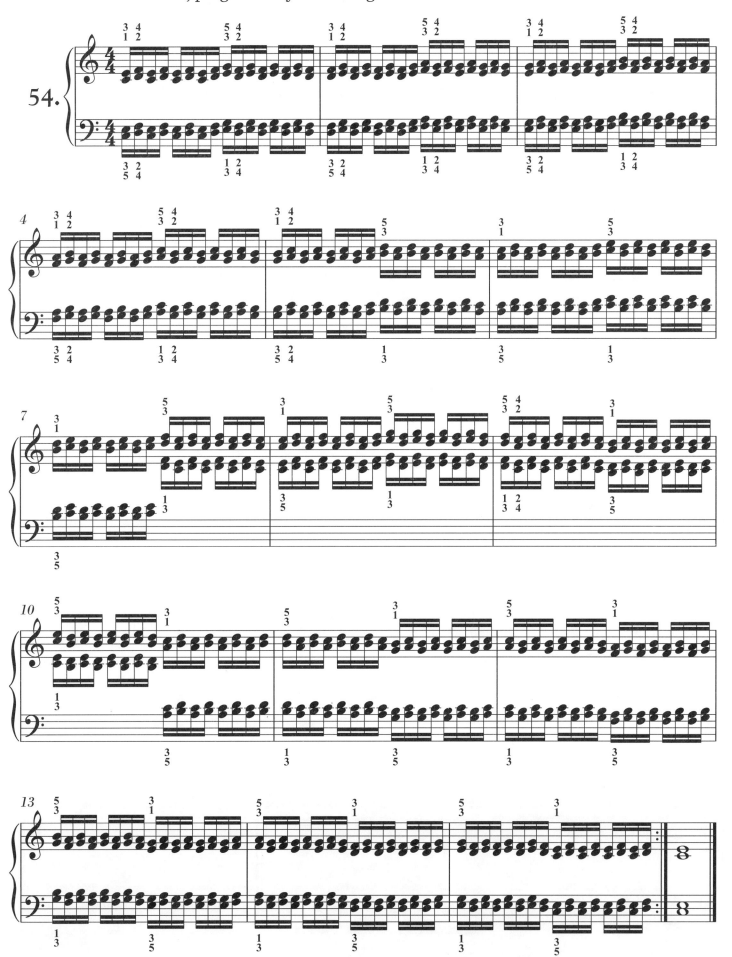

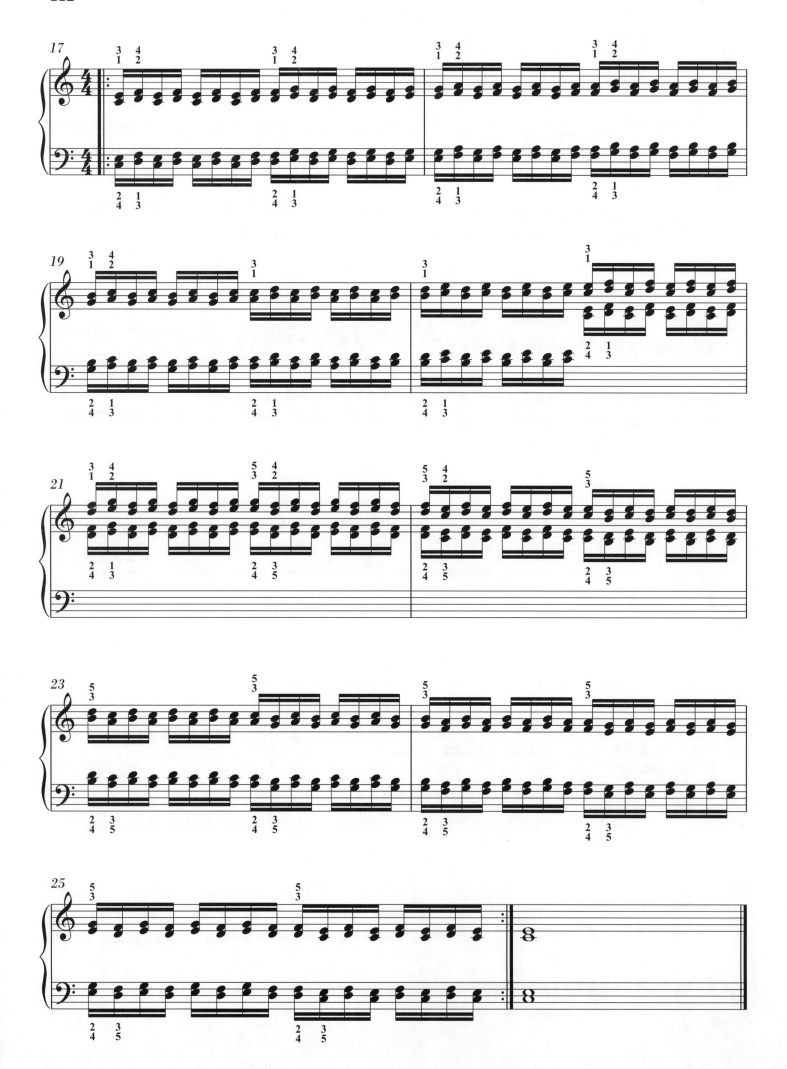

The triple trill.

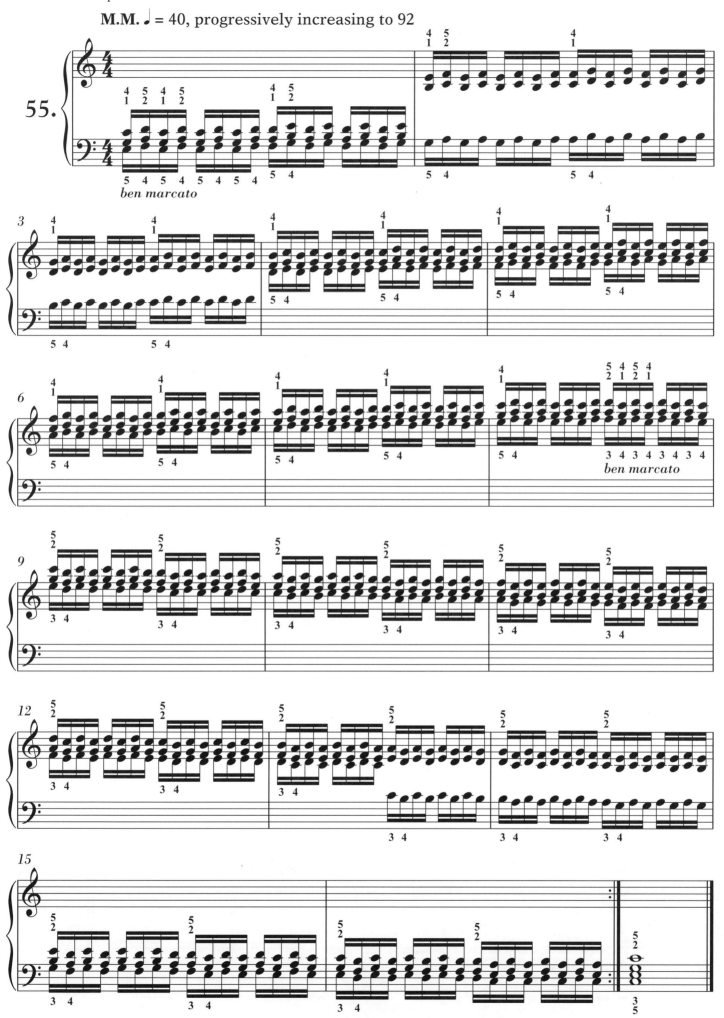

The quadruple trill.

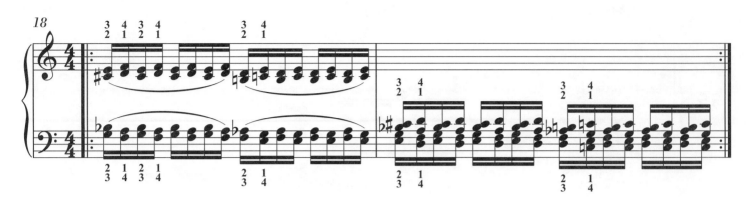

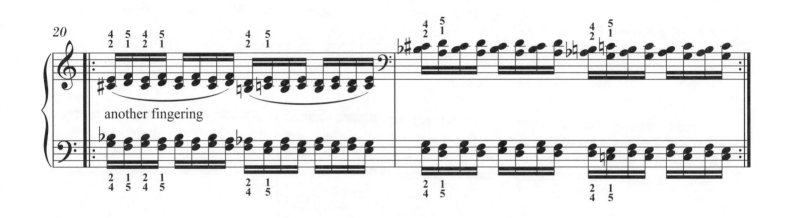

another fingering

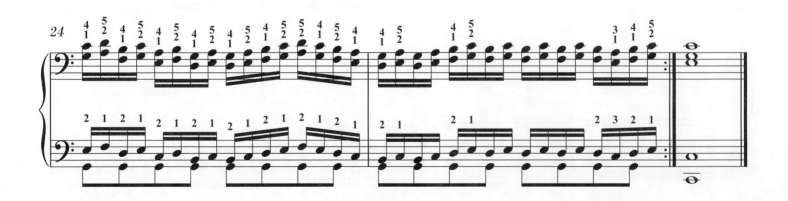

Broken Octave Scales in the 24 Keys

To be played without stopping. This exercise is of great importance in preparing the wrists for the study of the tremolo.

M.M. ♩ = 60, progressively increasing to 120

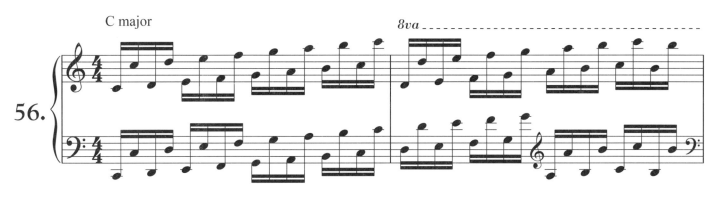

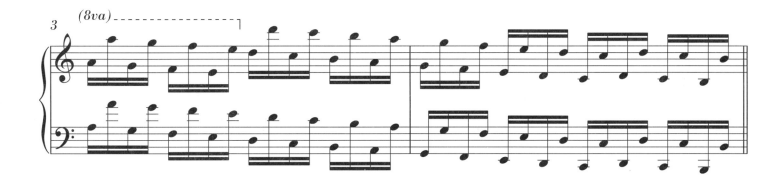

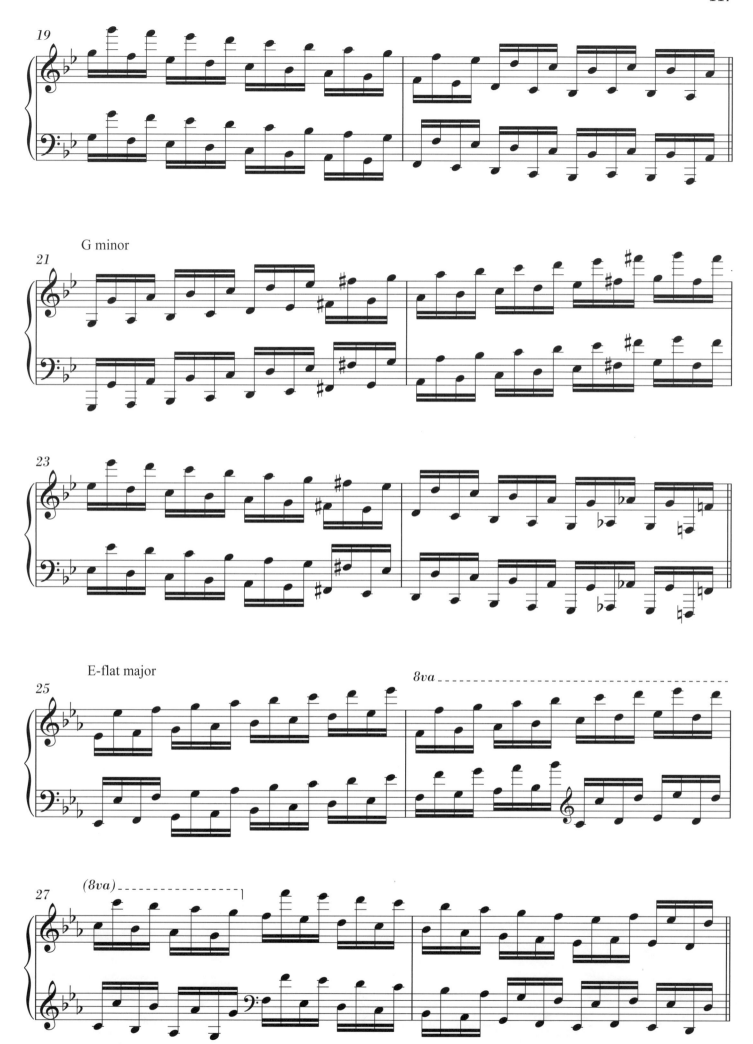

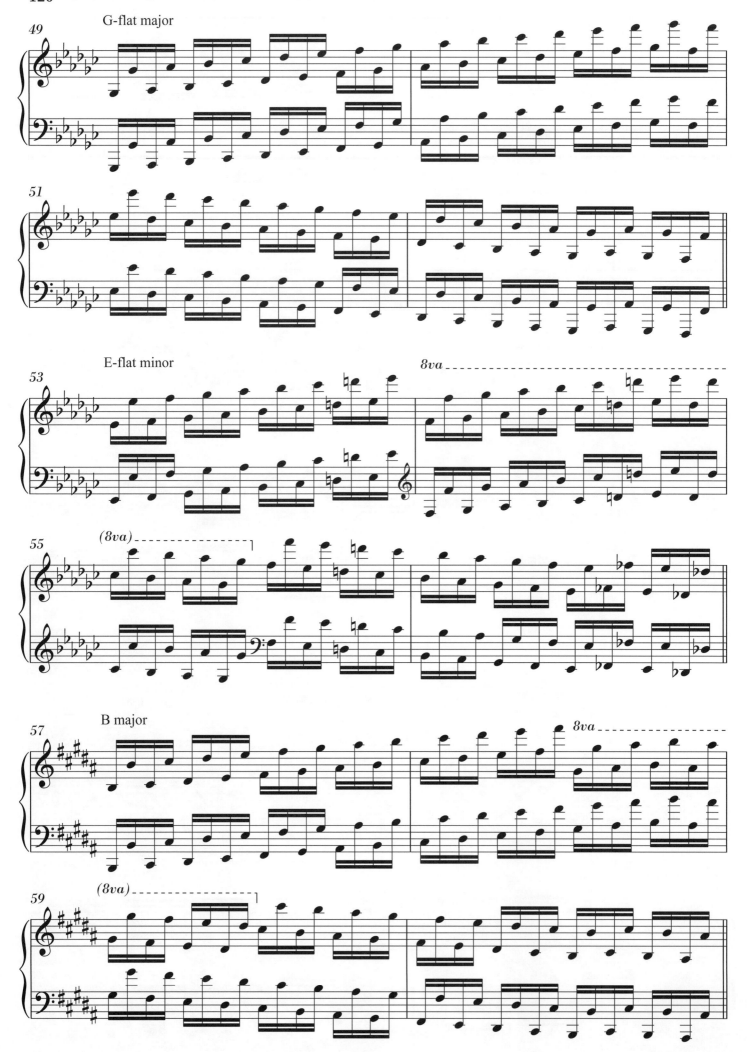

124

Arpeggios in Octaves in the 24 Keys

First practice the arpeggio in C and before moving to the next, make sure that it is played properly and clearly. Then practice the 24 arpeggios, played without interruption, if possible.

M.M. ♩ = 40, progressively increasing to 72

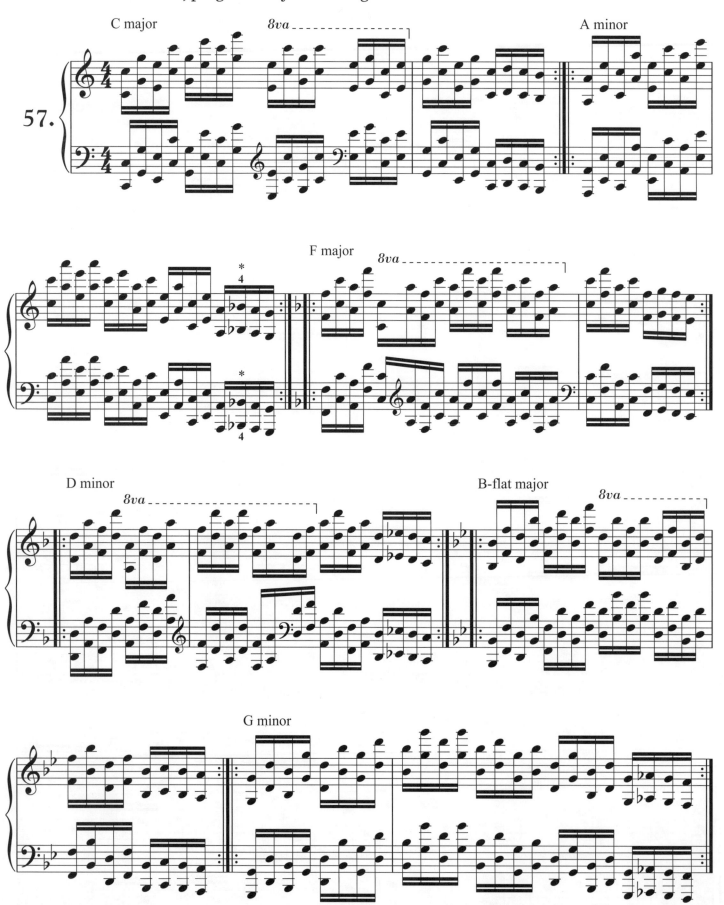

*In all of this exercise the black keys are to be played with the 4th finger of each hand.

125

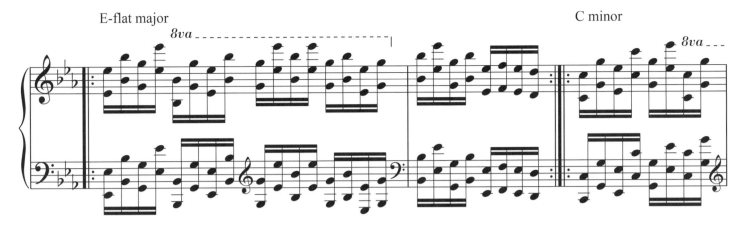

E-flat major

C minor

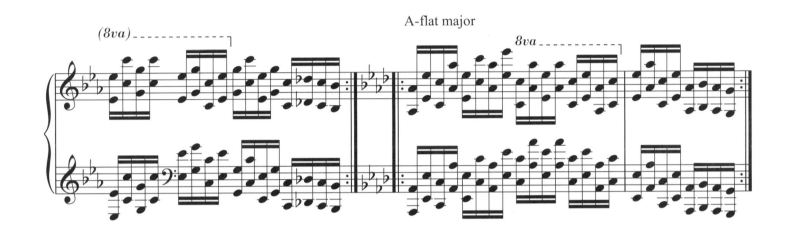

A-flat major

F minor

D-flat major

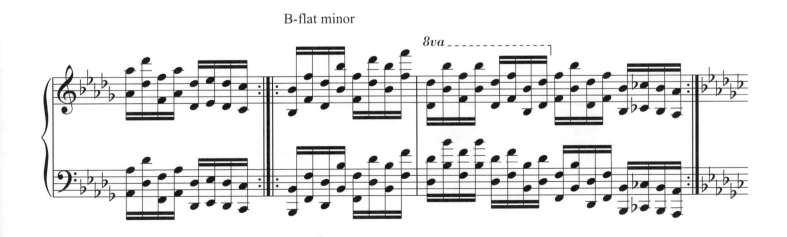

B-flat minor

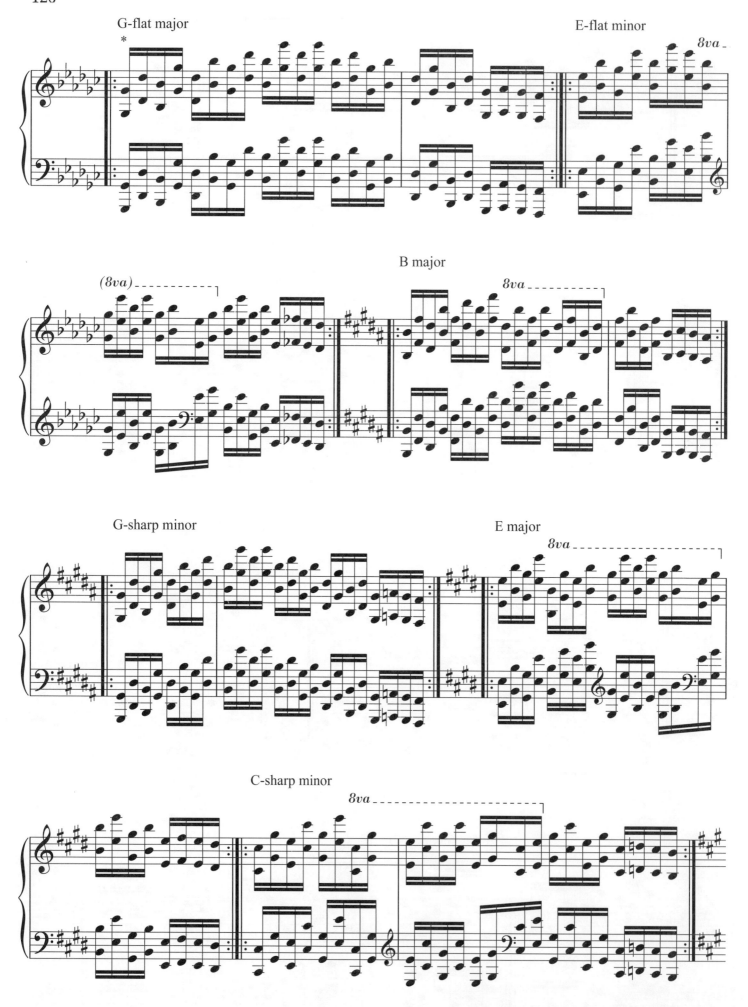

*As this arpeggio and the next one in E-flat minor are on black keys alone, it makes no difference whether the 4th or 5th finger be employed.

A major

F-sharp minor

D major

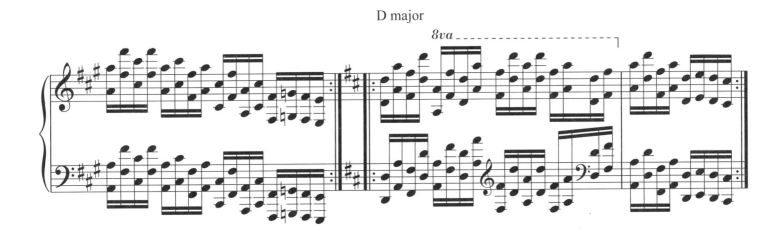

B minor

G major

E minor

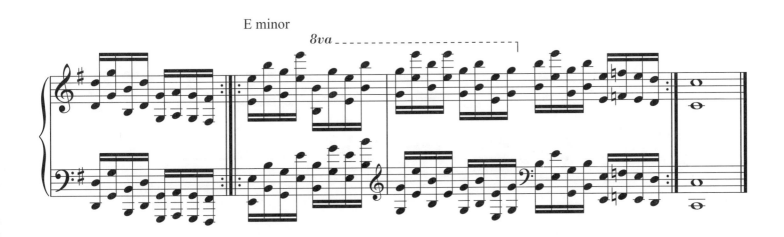

Held octaves (with accompanying detached notes). Vigorously play the octaves, holding without articulating the wrists. The internal notes should be played quickly with articulated fingers.

M.M. ♩ = 60, progressively increasing to 92

Quadruple trill in sixths, for the combination of the 1st and 4th, and 2nd and 5th, fingers of each hand. Move neither hand nor wrist at all while playing this exercise.

M.M. ♩ = 40, progressively increasing to 84

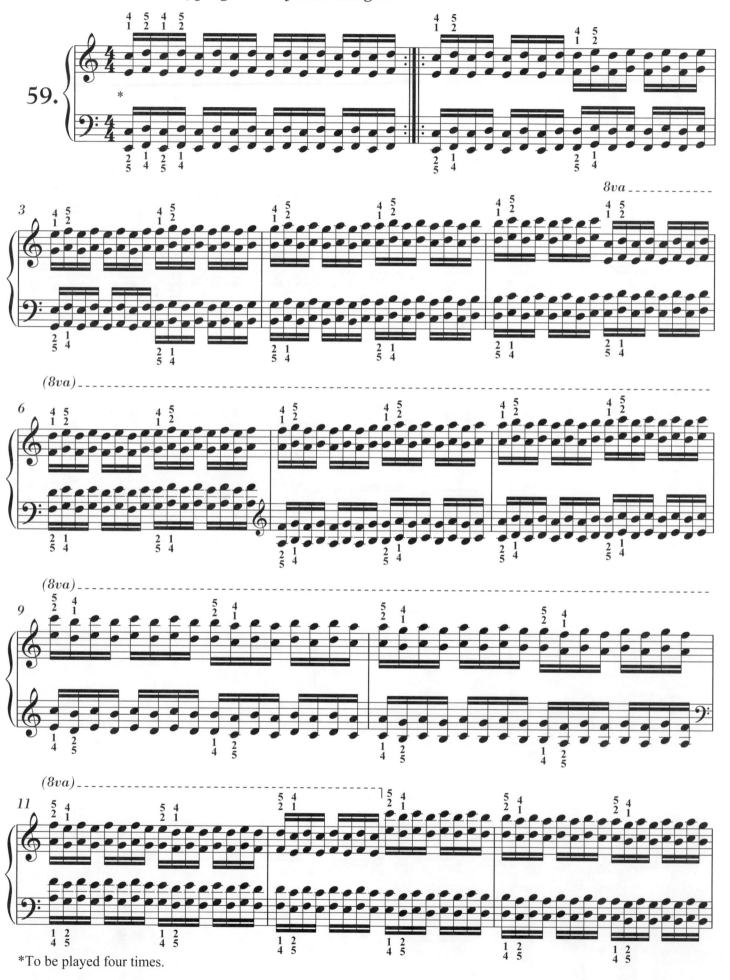

*To be played four times.

M.M. ♩ = 40, progressively increasing to 84

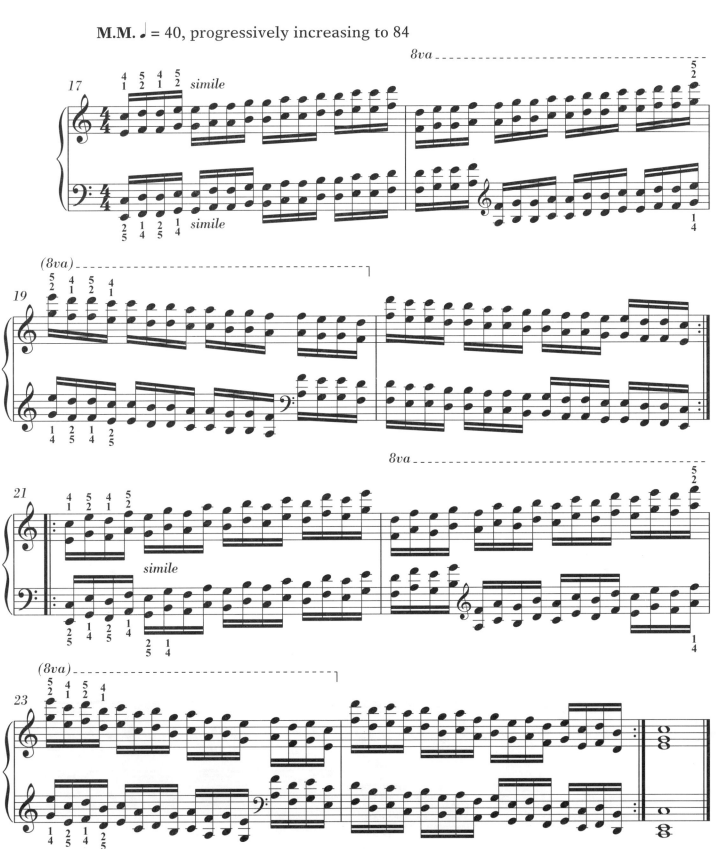

The Tremolo

To execute the tremolo, it must be given the speed of movement of a roll on the timpani. First play slowly, then gradually accelerate until the metronome indication of 72 is reached. Finally, by the oscillation of the wrists, increase the rapidity up to that of a drum roll. This exercise is long and difficult; but the excellence of the result largely compensates the pianist for the troubles and hardships imposed by pursuing it to the end.

M.M. ♩ = 48, progressively increasing to 72

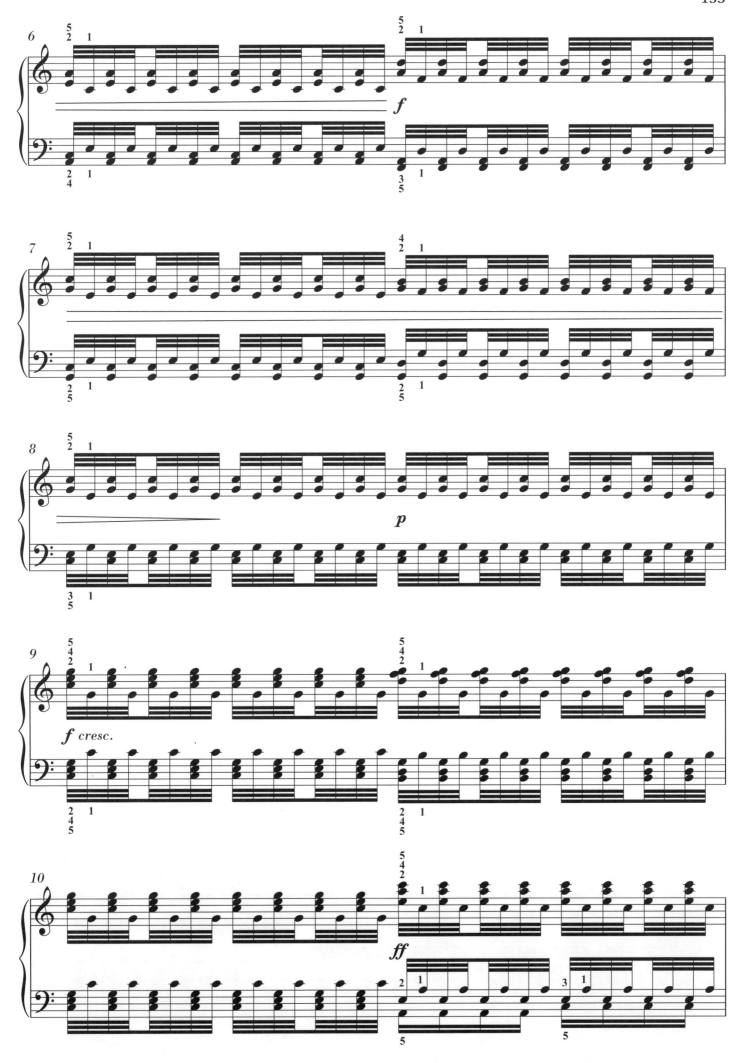

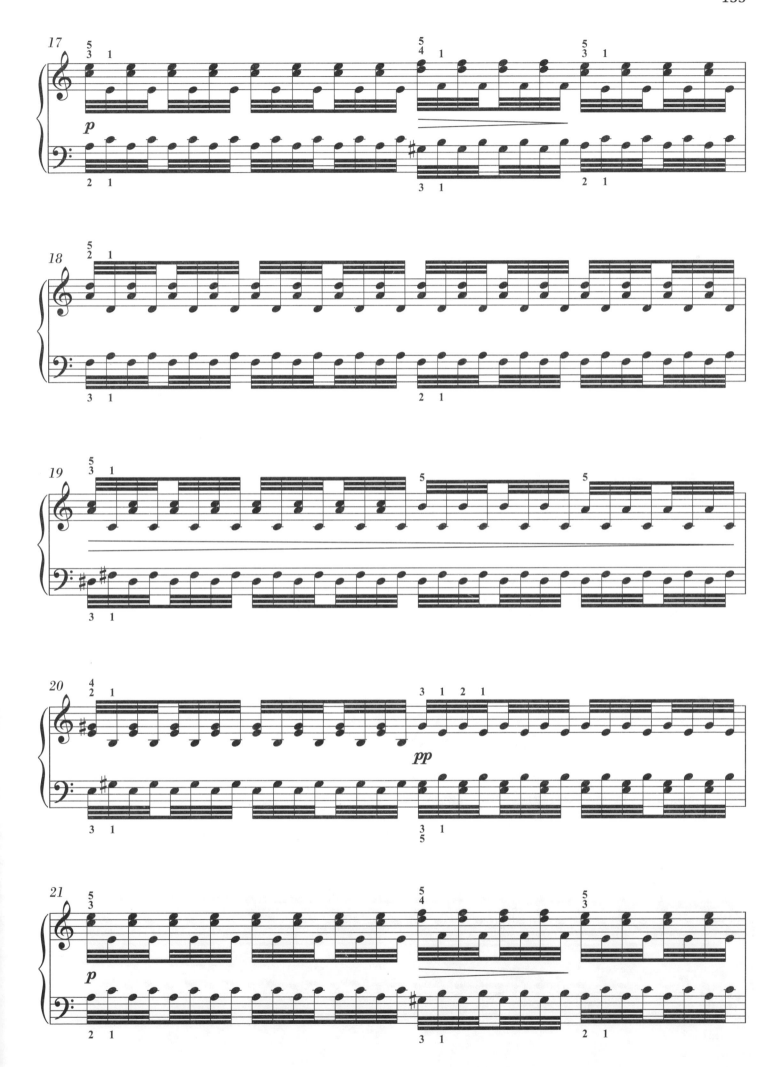

138

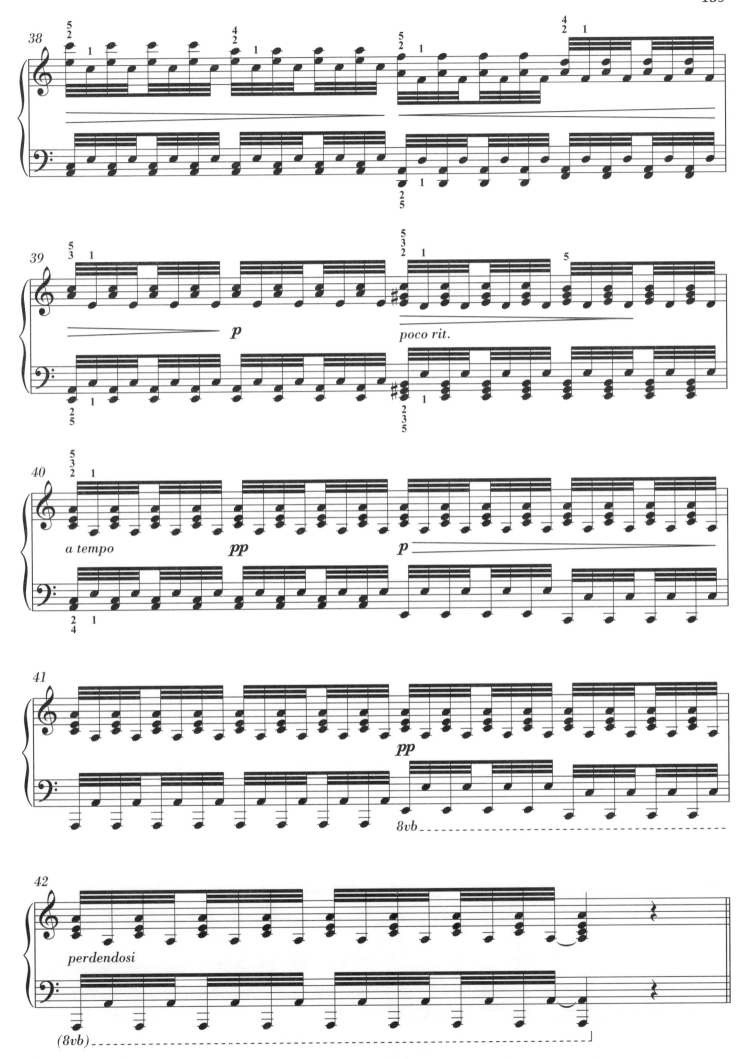

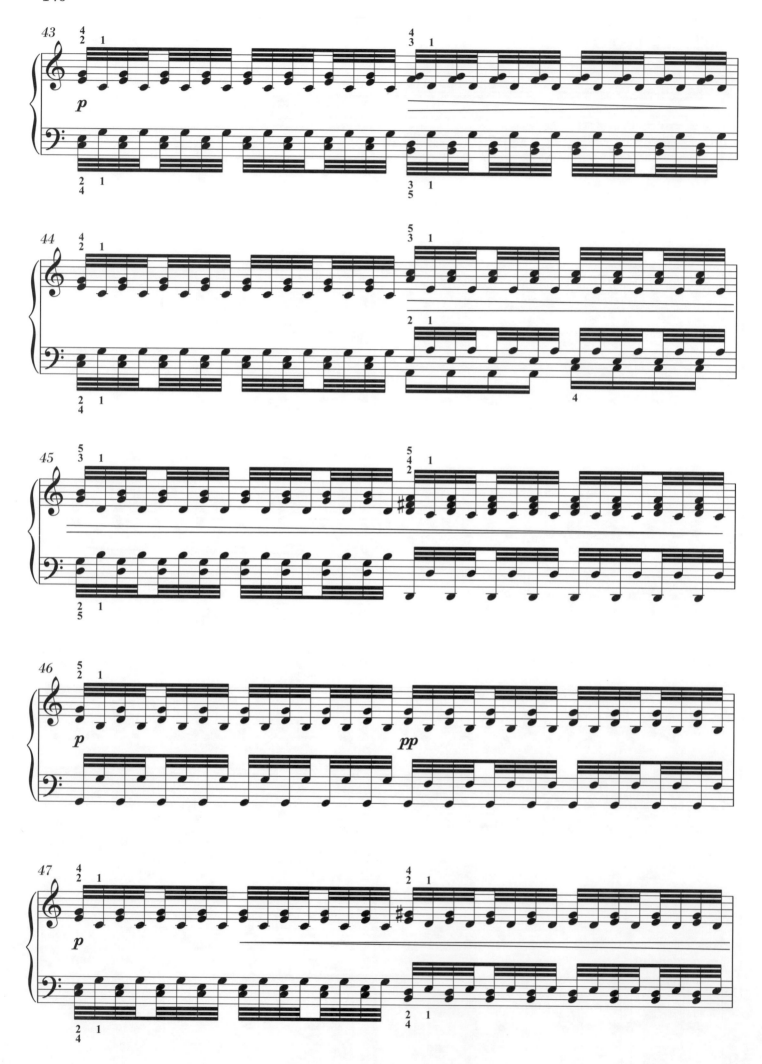

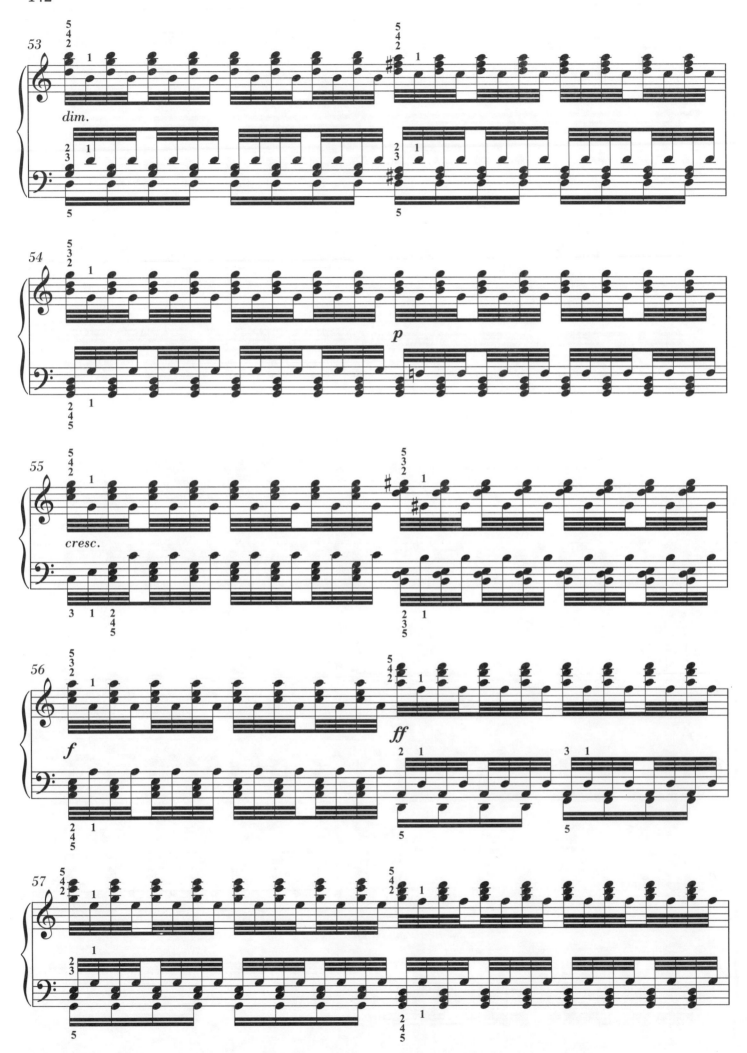

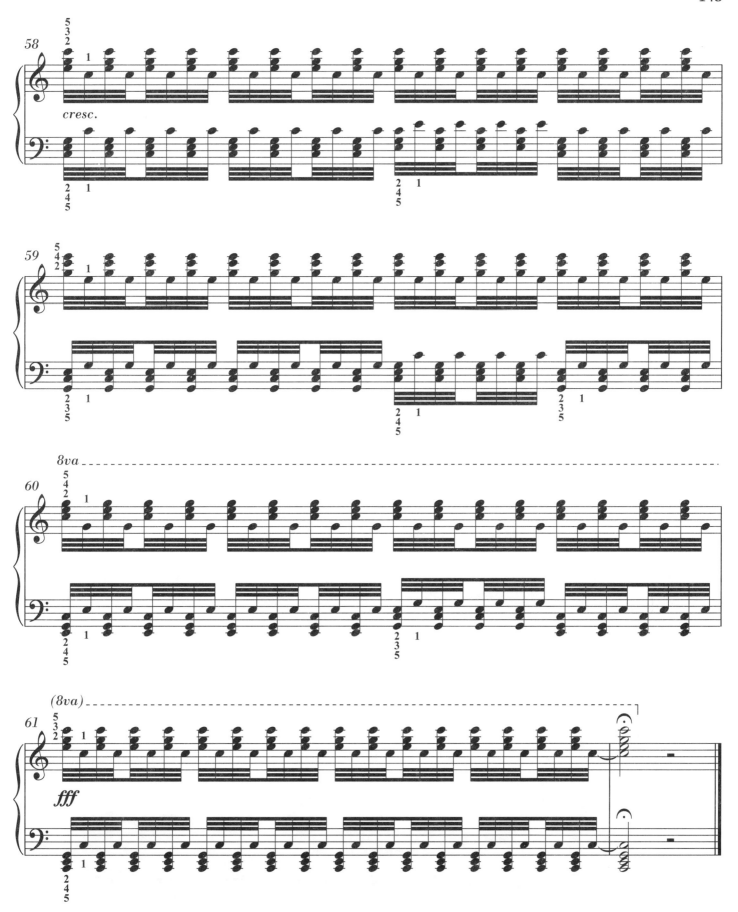

Conclusion

Now that the student has studied everything in this volume, he *[sic]* knows the greatest technical difficulties, but if he wants the fruit of his work and to become a true virtuoso, he must play this book piecemeal every day for 15 to 20 minutes. The great difficulties will then be made familiar. It is little work compared with the huge benefits that will result. The greatest artists are forced to repeat exercises daily and spend hours just for technical support for their talent. We cannot be called over-demanding if we ask the student to play the greatest possible number of these exercises every day.